Dead Snails Leave No Trails

DEAD SNAILS LEAVE NO TRAILS

REVISED

Natural Pest Control for Home and Garden

Loren Nancarrow

AND

Janet Hogan Taylor

TEN SPEED PRESS
Berkeley

Thank you to everyone who purchased the first edition of *Dead Snails Leave No Trails*. We hope you love this new and improved edition.

Thank you isn't enough to say to our agent, Julie Castiglia. You share our love of nature and understood our dream from the very beginning.

Copyright © 1996, 2013 by Loren Nancarrow and Janet Hogan Taylor

Published in the United States by Ten Speed Press, an imprint of the Crown Publishing Group, a division of Random House, Inc., New York.
www.crownpublishing.com
www.tenspeed.com

Ten Speed Press and the Ten Speed Press colophon are registered trademarks of Random House, Inc.

A previous edition was published by Ten Speed Press, Berkeley, CA, in 1996.

Library of Congress Cataloging-in-Publication Data
Nancarrow, Loren.
  Dead snails leave no trails : natural pest control for home and garden /
Loren Nancarrow and Janet Hogan Taylor. — Rev.
      p. cm.
  Natural pest control for home and garden
  Includes bibliographical references and index.
  1. Garden pests—Control. 2. Plants, Protection of. 3. Household pests—Control.
  I. Taylor, Janet Hogan, 1954- II. Title. III. Title: Natural pest control for home and garden.
  SB603.5.N36 2013
  635'.0496—dc23

Trade Paperback ISBN: 978-1-60774-319-4
eBook ISBN: 978-1-60774-320-0

Printed in the United States of America

Design by Colleen Cain
Illustrations by Janet Hogan Taylor

10 9 8 7 6 5 4 3 2 1

Revised Edition

Contents

Introduction

Take a stroll through most home-and-garden stores these days and it's easy to believe we've cured our addiction to chemicals. Terms like "organic," "earth friendly," "all natural," "locally grown," and so on are prominently displayed on product packaging. But our enlightenment may be more about slogans and marketing than a new understanding of the natural world and the importance of protecting it.

I realized how little we've moved toward chemical-free gardening while using social media. In addition to posting vacation pictures and keeping in touch with friends from back home, I use Facebook to share occasional gardening videos and images from my organic growing projects. Recently, I posted pictures of tomato hornworms, their sphinx moth mothers, and the cocoons containing the next generation of the hungry pests. My thinking was to connect the dots for gardeners who are suddenly finding the gigantic caterpillars in their gardens. Many people posted the inevitable: "Eewwww," "Yuck," and "Ohhh gross!" Quite a few people were surprised and appreciative that they now understood the pest's life stages.

Aha! I had them, and I wanted to relate it to the best and least-toxic way to kill the garden bad guys. So I posted a picture of a hornworm covered with eggs from the tiny beneficial braconid wasp and added a short blurb explaining what the picture showed. I also suggested they be left in the garden when found with the eggs on their backs.

Now, after sharing my views for more than thirty years on TV in California, I assume the people who "friend" me on Facebook know I advocate less toxic methods of feeding our plants and managing pests. So I was shocked at the responses to my latest caterpillar and parasite picture. Those who commented advocated everything up to and including nuclear attack to kill the hornworm and especially the one with the growths all over its back. I reasoned with them: "No, wait—if left alone the eggs will hatch, and the baby wasps will eat the caterpillar and go on to search and destroy any other caterpillars in the garden!" They didn't care. All they wanted was the thing gone; methods be damned. The last things they wanted were worms *and* wasps! Oh well, I tried. But I knew there had to be a better way—and that is precisely what my friend Janet Taylor and I hope to provide in the pages ahead.

Thank you for picking up *Dead Snails Leave No Trails*. Between these covers, Janet and I have compiled some unique ideas we've discovered to eliminate out-of-control pests. We also share some old-fashioned but logical methods of nonchemical gardening and pest control. Our goal is to consider how nature seeks balance. Infestations most often happen when that balance is upset, allowing single species to grow out of control. That's exactly what we face when chemical pesticides are used. They are indiscriminate killers. Chemical insect sprays do not understand the difference between an insect that will eat your prized veggies and the ones that make their living by eating the same insect pests you want gone. When exterminating sprays enter the equation, everything is killed, and it's the pests that return first and in greater numbers, followed much more slowly by the beneficial critters.

In an organically grown garden, balance is the general rule. Pests still exist, but so do the natural means of dealing with them. Unfortunately, in our efforts to harvest maximum amounts of food, we've come to view all insects as enemies. We have created chemical poisons to kill and chemical fertilizers to encourage growth. They each appear to achieve their objective, and in the case of chemical pesticides, they do their job too well. But again, most are indiscriminate and kill everything with which they come into contact. Too many of the victims are beneficial insects and animals, which perform the essential work of pollinating, breaking down organic matter, and killing pests. Our goal is to replicate nature when possible or to use the least toxic means of achieving our goal of a happy, healthy, natural home and garden.

My coauthor Janet is an entomologist by profession. Her knowledge of the insect world still astounds me, twenty years after we first met. She is the brains in this operation and knows more about the creepy crawlers in our homes and gardens than any ordinary person could ever hope to know. On the other hand, I turned my gardening hobby into part of my profession as a way to maintain sanity. As a southern California TV weatherman, I was going crazy. All those jokes are true. The weather is wonderful, but most days are between 65°F and 70°F, with night and morning low clouds and afternoon sunshine. The rest of the time there are either raging east winds that spark destructive wildfires or brief heavy downpours that cause hillsides to give way in the famous western mudslides.

Most of the year I was bored silly, repeating the same numbers and conditions day in and day out. When I began adding short segments on the native animals in my yard, or the ants that I found had invaded my kitchen counter, I was happily shocked by the response. People related. Some had wondered about the same creature in their yard or had awakened to the same ant invasion. When I met Janet, she said she'd noticed the TV segments and thought we should team up. Together, we've learned so much about the things that bug us, and together we've come up with some highly effective ways to foil pests and encourage the good guys. We hope you'll agree that a chemical-free yard and garden, where nature is in balance, is a much nicer place to be.

—Loren Nancarrow

chapter one

Pesticide Savvy
(Synthetic vs. Natural vs. Biological)

For as long as humankind has existed, insects have generally been regarded as pests. But to be a true "pest," an organism must do one of the following: damage crops, destroy products, transmit diseases, stand in the way of human interests or needs, or simply become annoying. To achieve the goal of eradicating pests, chemical pesticides have been developed to battle the invaders. (A *pesticide* is defined as any chemical that is intended to kill pests.) Pesticides can be man-made or derived from plants, and care must be taken with all of them. Many scientists believe that no insect pest species has ever been completely eradicated by the use of chemical pesticides, and, in some cases, pest species have become even more of a problem as a result of pesticide use.

Synthetic pesticides are man-made chemicals produced for the sole purpose of killing insect pests and other pests, such as weeds. These chemicals are produced in many forms for different applications. They can be sprayed or dusted on plants and animals or made into pellets and gaseous forms for application to the soil. The two major groups of synthetic pesticides are chlorinated hydrocarbons (such as DDT) and organo-phosphates (such as malathion).

Chlorinated hydrocarbon compounds date back to 1874, and they have been under great scrutiny in recent years. These compounds were once thought to be miracle cures for many plant pest problems throughout the world. They were used widely to treat everything from lice in Italy (DDT was credited with halting a typhus epidemic carried by lice) to the common cockroach in US homes. Problems arose from some of the residual effects of these compounds; for example, DDT has been linked to such problems as thinning of shells in some birds' eggs. Some of the target insects of these chemicals, such as cockroaches and flies, have even become resistant or immune to them.

Organo-phosphates are basically contact insecticides that were discovered in the course of poison gas research around the time of World War II. Some of these compounds are very toxic to humans and animals as well as to insects. A real danger of many of these compounds is that, in addition to the usual methods of contamination—breathing them in or eating them—they can also be absorbed directly through the skin. Malathion is one of the most-used organo-phosphates because it has a very short residual effect in the environment and is also less toxic to non-pest animals. Many species of insects that are resistant to chlorinated hydrocarbon pesticides will be killed by malathion.

In any case, great care must be taken when using any pesticide, should you decide to use one. Always read the label carefully, and follow the directions for applying the pesticide correctly. Pesticide labeling is based on research; it is provided for everyone's safety. It is actually against the law to not follow a pesticide label. It's wise to wear full protective clothing during application because nearly all pesticides are absorbed through the skin. The label will instruct you about what minimal protective clothing is required.

Natural controls are elements occurring physically in nature that help keep insect numbers in check. Such controls are found in every backyard and in all parts of the world. Some examples of natural controls are weather conditions, rainfall levels, the amount of shade in an area, and geographic location. For example, if you live in Alaska, the temperature will keep many tropical insects from taking up residence in your backyard. A wide river might keep a hopping insect from getting to your garden, but it might also be a breeding ground for mosquitoes. People have little effect on natural controls, but in today's age of jets and cars, many unwanted insects have found their way to a new home with unwitting human help.

Biological controls involve those living things that keep insect populations in check. Insect predators, including toads, frogs, moles, birds, and predatory insects, are a good example. Many naturally occurring diseases, caused by viruses, fungi, and bacteria, also keep insect populations down. It is in this area of natural checks and balances where humans have often upset the balance of beneficial and destructive insects.

A pest-management method called *biological control* or *biocontrol* allows the introduction or augmentation of predatory insects, parasites, or diseases in a pest area in order to reduce the population of a specific pest. This method works best on large one-crop parcels where there is generally one major pest. A good example of this is the introduction of *vedalia*, an Australian ladybug beetle, to control cottony-cushion scale, a pest of citrus trees.

Some biological controls that are not so species-specific are gaining popularity among gardeners and farmers alike. One of these is a bacterium called *Bacillus thuringiensis* (Bt). It attacks many species of caterpillars, including tomato hornworms and gypsy moths. Biological controls generally do not completely eliminate a pest, but a natural balance will occur once the control agent becomes established. Biological controls will continue to control the target pest year after year and may only occasionally need to be augmented. But keep in mind that biological controls do not work overnight. Predators and parasites take time to become established, and insect diseases and pathogens take time to spread and infect new victims. It's difficult to sit back and watch your garden being fed upon when you've just treated it with a biological control, but if you give the controls time to take hold, the rewards will be well worth it.

INTEGRATED PEST MANAGEMENT

Back in the 1970s, the practice of eradicating pests with chemicals came under fire when studies discovered that shells of bird eggs were thinning and questions were raised about the environmental impact of using chemicals. The term "integrated pest management" (IPM) was coined to describe a new method for controlling pests in crops and gardens. IPM is basically a pest management strategy that looks at all aspects of pest management and comes up with a comprehensive analysis of the problem to produce the maximum crop yield and the minimum adverse effects to humans and the environment.

The first step in IPM is to choose healthy plants and give them the best growing conditions possible. Next, use all the available information about crop rotation, elimination of pest host plants, timed plantings, and timed harvests to reduce the severity of crop damage due to pests. After that, if an insect or disease does become a problem, the next step is physically controlling the pest. Physical control includes handpicking, traps, and barrier methods. If those controls fail, biological controls are added to the program. Finally, if all else fails, chemical controls are used as the last resort.

A planting journal is a great tool to track this information. List planting dates, when and what type of pests appear, methods of control, and so on. This allows for year-to-year planning. Integrated pest management is based on the knowledge that some damage will occur—the secret of IPM is to know when to act on a problem pest. Many truly organic gardeners agree with this practice up to the point that chemical measures are used. IPM techniques are mainly commonsense approaches, so it's likely that most people have used some form of integrated pest management in their own gardens at one time or another.

In the following chapters, you'll find many ideas for your own integrated pest management program. Tailor the program to your own specific problems and needs by observing your garden carefully to understand which insects are pests and which are beneficial. Check our Resources and Buying Guide section on page 166 for more guidance. These are valuable resources for you in your quest to discover "What's eating my plants?"

PESTICIDE SAFETY

When all else has failed and you feel you must use a pesticide, the following guidelines will help you use the pesticide safely. Remember that even relatively nontoxic pesticides can cause problems if used improperly.

- When choosing a pesticide, choose a product that is registered (government-approved) for your problem pest. Don't try to kill everything with a broad-spectrum pesticide. Be certain the product you choose is intended for the pest and pest life stage you are trying to control.

- Always read the entire label and follow it exactly. Never add more of the chemical than the label calls for. The label is a legal document that tells you everything you need to know when using that product. It spells out exactly the characteristics of the pesticide and its proper use.

- If you have children or pets, store the pesticides in a locked cabinet. Keep the telephone number of the nearest poison control center in the cabinet and by your phone. Never remove the label from the container or pour a chemical into another container that does not have the same chemical label attached to it. You will need this label to tell the doctor exactly what your child or pet got into. Sometimes antidote information is given on the label.

- Wear gloves when handling and mixing the pesticide, and remember that many pesticides can be absorbed through the skin. Always mix a pesticide in a well-ventilated area. The precautionary statement on the pesticide label usually gives important information on the hazards of the pesticide as well as the instructions for handling it. This statement also explains any toxicity to other organisms, such as bees or fish.

- Buy only what you need for the current problem. Some products break down over time, and you will not be treating your problem properly if you use a pesticide that has been stored for a long time.

- Spot treatment is better for the environment than a full-scale assault. Use the pesticide on the smallest area possible, keeping in mind that many pesticides kill beneficial insects as well as harmful ones.

- Apply the pesticide when the pest is most vulnerable. If you have to use a pesticide, it's best to do so when it will be most effective. For example, spraying caterpillars, which can't move quickly, will be more effective than trying to spray the flying adults.

- Never apply a spray-type pesticide when it is windy. Most pesticide companies recommend not spraying when the wind is over five miles per hour. Early morning spraying usually works best.
- Never smoke, eat, or drink when applying pesticides, or allow anyone else to do so in the application area.

PESTICIDE INFORMATION RESOURCES

Your local county agriculture department, farm bureau, or agricultural (cooperative) extension office all have websites and offices. Check the government pages of your local telephone directory for phone numbers.

National Pesticide Telecommunications Network
(800) 858-PEST or (800) 858-7378
This agency is sponsored by the EPA and Oregon State University.
Go online for objective science-based information about pesticides and information on integrated pest management, food safety, and even pest identification at www.npic.orst.edu.

American Association of Poison Control Centers
Their website, www.aapcc.org, is filled with good information. If you prefer, call them with questions at (800) 222-1222.

US Environmental Protection Agency
Ariel Rios Building
1200 Pennsylvania Avenue, NW
Washington, DC 20460
(202) 272-0167
Go online or check your phone directory for regional offices. The EPA website has good information on various topics related to the environment: www.epa.gov.

chapter two

Home Pest Control

ANTS

You wake up one morning to find ants all over your kitchen counter. Ants are very opportunistic, and no matter how clean your home seems to be, they'll keep coming back by the thousands. Don't worry—help is on the way.

Ant eradication ideas and recipes

To get rid of the ants you see, spray a soapy water mixture or commercial window cleaner on the ants and their trail. Any cleaner with ammonia, alcohol, soap, or pure citrus extract will work, or you can make your own Ammonia Solution (see page 13). It will kill the ants and break their trail (and clean your counters at the same time).

You can also combat ants by sending poison back to their nest with them. Our simple Indoor Ant Bait (see page 13) is an effective method. This mixture of borax (or boric acid—sold as roach bait—which is very inexpensive and available at most home and garden centers) and corn syrup can work wonders on ants that enjoy a sweet dinner. **Warning:** Boric acid is a liver and kidney toxin which, over time, can make children and pets sick. A small one-time dose will most likely cause only an upset stomach; however, if your pet is showing worrisome signs of distress, contact the poison control center in your area. Grease ants, which love oily foods, will ignore this bait. If you find your ants are the grease-hungry kind, try the Ant Death Bait recipe on page 35—and mix the dry ingredients with lard or shortening until the mixture is crumbly. Make sure you keep this away from pets by placing the crumbly mixture in a small plastic container in which holes have been punched along the bottom to allow the ants access.

Baking soda mixed with sugar makes great ant and roach bait (see the Sweet Roach Bait recipe on page 22). Place a tablespoon or so of each in an empty spice bottle with a shaker top. You want to be able to lay the bottle down on its side without having the contents spill out. Place the bottle where you have seen ants or where you think ants are getting into your home, so the ants can go in but the bottle keeps your pets out.

> Sure, *you* can say a lot with a kiss, but ants can say even more! They communicate by exchanging chemicals in their mouths.

If you can, follow the ants back to their nest. Here you can also use the Ant Death Bait in dry form or the Sweet Roach Bait. Sprinkle a thin layer of either bait evenly around the nest opening. (Don't make piles that dogs can lick up, as they love sugar.) For easy application, mix the bait with powdered sugar and use a sifter to apply. (You should reserve an old sifter for this purpose; don't use the same one you use for baking.) The ants will carry the mixture into the nest to feed to the colony, killing those that eat it. Repeat the sprinkling as long as you see ants.

Now that you have found the problem nest, here are a few more options:

- Pour boiling water on the nest to kill the beasts. It won't kill all the ants at one time, but after a few repeated treatments it should really cut down on their numbers.

- A strong Chile Solution (see the recipe on page 13) poured into the nest will not only kill the ants but also make the nest unlivable.

- Sprinkle cornmeal around the ants' mound opening. The ants eat the dry cornmeal, which expands inside their bodies and kills them.

Repelling ants

There are several ways to prevent ants from becoming a problem in the first place. One of these ideas might be the solution for you:

- Follow any ant trails to your home's entry point (such as holes in the wall or floor) and plug the holes.

- Try using mentholated rub, but be sure to test a spot to make sure it won't stain.

- Dab a little eucalyptus oil, citrus oil, or lemon juice on a rag and wipe it in your cupboards or entry points. You can also soak a string in the oil and stuff it into holes or along a crack.

- Use talcum powder, cayenne pepper, cinnamon, or boric acid powder (see warning, page 10) to sprinkle in windows. Ants do not like to cross powdery substances. Replace if it gets wet.

- Cucumber peels are also thought to have a repellent quality for ants.

- Mint tea leaves or cloves left in areas where you find ants can repel them. Replace when the scent is gone.

- One report states that leaving a light on in the kitchen or bathroom when you are having a problem there with ants can change their foraging habits.

- Sprinkle food-grade diatomaceous earth around the perimeter of a house or garden. For ants, trying to cross this substance is like walking on broken glass. Like the other powders suggested, it must be replaced if it gets wet. Avoid using swimming pool diatomaceous earth (see page 92). **Warning:** When using diatomaceous earth, *always* wear a protective dust mask to avoid inhaling any potentially harmful particles, and *never* dust when children and pets are present.

Know your ant enemy

Ants are members of the wasp class of insects. There are more than 3,500 species of ants living in nearly every habitat around the world. All of these ants are social and live in colonies called nests or mounds. The colony consists of a queen and female workers. When a nest gets overcrowded (some nests have over a million ants), the queen will produce winged males and females that go out and establish new nests.

Ammonia Solution

1 pint water
1 tablespoon ammonia

Mix and spray on counters and windows.

Alcohol Solution

Combine equal parts water, isopropyl alcohol, and white vinegar.
Spray on counters and windows. (Bonus: This leaves a nice shine
with no streaks.)

Indoor Ant Bait

9 teaspoons light corn syrup
1 teaspoon boric acid (see warning, page 10) or borax

Combine the ingredients. Place one drop of the mixture on a post-
age stamp-sized piece of cardboard and place it where you see
ants. Let the ants swarm the bait and take it back to the nest, where
they will eat it and feed it to their young. The ants prefer fresh bait
and tend to ignore bait that is dried, so you may need to replace it
periodically.

Hot Chile Solution

Quart jar
2 to 4 sliced hot chiles (serrano, habanero, or jalapeño
   work well)

Put the sliced chiles into the jar and fill with hot water. Let the mixture steep for at least 24 hours. Remove the peppers and pour the
solution into the nest.

Different species of ants, looking for different foods, can invade your home at the same time. The pale pharaoh ant searches for fatty foods; the thief ant prefers protein foods.

Scent trails left behind by a scout ant provide a chemical connection between the nest and a food source, like your kitchen. The trail lasts for only a few minutes, but that's usually long enough for the ants to get from the nest to the food.

Scientists have demonstrated that ants are capable of individual learning and of passing on what they have learned. They have demonstrated the ability to remember and recall and to correct their mistakes, which explains why they can be so hard to get rid of.

BEDBUGS

Bedbugs used to be the source of old jokes, but no one is laughing now. The number of incidences of bedbug infestations has skyrocketed in recent years. Even going to the movies or changing in a dressing room has the potential of bringing the dreaded bugs back to your home.

How do I know I have them?

Bedbugs are small but can be seen with the naked eye. Adults are reddish-brown to a darker brown and about a quarter of an inch long. Bedbug bodies are oval-shaped and flattened, which allows them to slip between cracks and bedding.

Bedbugs feed on blood, and generally the first sign of a bedbug is that something has bitten you. Often people think the bite is from a flea and do not think much about it until populations of the bedbugs build up and they are really getting bitten. The bite is actually a puncture caused by the bug's piercing mouthparts, much like a mosquito bite. Bedbugs are not considered disease carriers, but the bites are certainly bad enough. Some people can develop a skin rash after a bedbug bite, and the bites can be quite itchy. To determine whether you have them, look for the bugs' excrement or fecal matter, which will appear as dark or rusty spots on mattresses, bedding, or furniture. Check all of the following, using a flashlight and magnifying glass if necessary:

- All joints and cracks in bed frames, headboards, or bed platforms. You may need to dismantle these to get into every crack.
- Mattresses, top and bottom, especially along the seams
- Behind baseboards, switch plates, pictures, and so on
- Under carpet edges, along tack strips and baseboards
- Furniture seams and crevices
- Any dark place in the house

What can I do to get rid of them?

Early detection will really help. Once you suspect bedbugs, don't wait—attack them now. If you don't want to use pesticides, you can try some of these ideas, but bedbugs will move when disturbed, so eliminating them is often a whole house effort:

- Mattress and box spring covers—some are certified to completely seal a mattress so the bedbugs are trapped. Follow manufacturer's recommendations, but be aware that generally it will take a year to completely kill all bedbugs inside the cover because bedbugs can live a year without feeding.
- Vacuum like crazy. Pour a quarter cup of boric acid (see warning, page 10) or borax into your lint cup or vacuum bag. This will kill any bedbugs you vacuum up. Use your crevice tool to vacuum every nook and cranny you can find. Make sure you vacuum everything in the room, including dresser drawers, closets, furniture, under beds, along baseboards, carpets—everything. Discard the vacuum bags in a sealed plastic bag.
- Wash everything that is washable—clothes, pillows, and so on—in the hottest water and dry on the highest setting that is safe for the fabric. Fabrics that can't be washed can be put in the dryer on the highest setting that is safe.
- Wash solid surfaces—headboards, dressers, floors, and so on.
- Check the whole house every week for any signs of the bugs.

What if cleaning and vacuuming aren't enough?

You may need to use pesticides. There are several home-use dusts and sprays that can be purchased by the homeowner. When using any product that contains dust particles, *always* wear a protective dust mask to avoid inhaling any potentially harmful particles, and *never* dust when children and pets are present. Foggers are *not* recommended, because they are thought to spread the bugs. Many products are designed for bedding, furniture, and household items. Always check the manufacturer's label and follow it exactly. Note: For maximum effectiveness, many professionals recommend treating affected areas three times, ten days apart.

If the task is just too much for you, it's time to call in the professionals. Professional exterminators will complete a thorough inspection and recommend a course of action. These measures may include pesticides, cleaning, or a combination of both. Some companies also do heat treatment. Studies have shown that bedbugs can be killed in seven minutes when heated to 115°F. To apply this treatment, heaters are brought into your home and the temperature raised enough to kill the bugs.

Can I prevent getting bedbugs?

Being aware of bedbugs and how easily they can hitchhike a ride to your home is the key, but sometimes that isn't good enough.

- Always check hotel rooms and luggage when traveling. Sprays can be purchased to kill bedbugs on luggage.
- Vacuum out luggage after traveling.
- Use caution when purchasing used beds or furniture. Some local pesticide companies can fumigate items for extra assurance.
- If you or your children come home with a bite, check your clothing carefully and place it directly into the washer. Don't take any chances.

Bedbug basics

Bedbugs are parasitic insects that belong to the insect family Cimicidae. The common bedbug *Cimex lectularius* prefers to feed on human blood. Bedbugs got their name because they like to feed where their victim likes to sleep. They have been pests of humans for thousands of years, but in developed areas their populations were greatly reduced and seldom seen in modern times. Many scientists think that world travel and pesticide resistance has caused the populations to rise.

Bedbugs are about a quarter of an inch in length and often mistaken for booklice or carpet beetles. When bedbugs hatch, they undergo five nymph stages before becoming adults. These nymphs look just like the adults but are smaller and lighter in color. Bedbugs communicate using pheromones or chemicals. These chemicals tell other bedbugs where there are nesting locations and feeding areas, and where to find a mate. Bedbugs seek out carbon dioxide and warmth to find their hosts.

Bedbug usually feed every five to ten days. It takes them about five to ten minutes to completely engorge themselves, much like a tick. We know from studies that bedbugs can go up to one year without feeding, but the average life span is closer to five months.

BROWN MARMORATED STINK BUGS

The invasion has begun. The brown marmorated stink bug from Asia was first found in the United States in 1998 in Allentown, Pennsylvania. Since that time the bug has spread within the United States and is causing an uproar, as the insects have become a year-round pest. They attack crops and gardens in warm months but what most people don't like is that they look for shelter in homes and buildings in colder months.

A stinky mess

When people find a large population of stink bugs in their home or garage, what they usually see is a stinky mess. When the homeowner tries to move them, they emit an odor—hence their common name. Because this is an introduced insect, they don't have many predators to keep their numbers down, so they are procreating unchecked. Their habit of migrating and accumulating en mass during the late fall and winter is common to other insects like ladybugs. What can you do besides live with the little stinkers?

Look carefully at your home's foundation, windows, doors, or eaves to identify any entry holes the insects could use to gain entry; these must be sealed or screened off. Remember, if these fairly large insects can get in, so can other more harmful insects like termites. You may need to place a tightly woven screen material, like that used for screening windows, over venting areas to prevent the insects from gaining entry. Use caulk to seal around windows and doors. If you must purchase a pesticide for this purpose, check product labels carefully and look for one that specifically lists stink bugs.

Once the insects are inside your home, a tried-and-true method is the vacuum cleaner. A canister vacuum with bags or a shop vacuum with a liner works bests. A small handheld vacuum can work if it has good suction. Before vacuuming the insects, first vacuum up a few tablespoons of boric acid (see warning, page 10) or powered insecticide to help kill the captured insects. If you don't have boric acid or powered insecticide, vacuuming can still be effective, but the added ingredient helps. A cold day also helps, because the insects are cold-blooded and move slowly, if at all, when cold. Vacuum up the insects, then take your vacuum outdoors. Quickly remove the vacuum bag or liner, place it in a plastic garbage bag, and seal it. Place the plastic garbage bag in the freezer for several hours or, even better, overnight. If the temperature outside is below freezing, just leave the bag outside. Once the insects are dead, throw them away.

Cracks and crevices and the area behind baseboards can be a haven for the unwanted invaders. Boric acid is effective here, too. It takes months to break down if it stays dry. Powders that work like razor blades to insects are talcum or talc-based baby powder and food-grade diatomaceous earth (see warning, page 12). Most insects will die if they get the powder on them. The downside to most powders is they all must be reapplied if they get wet.

There are several traps on the market that use pheromones or light to attract stink bugs to a trap. Entomologists have used light traps for years, and they can be made by anyone. One simple trap uses a large piece of white plastic sheeting. The size of the sheeting can vary, but it must be large enough to place a lamp or other lighting source behind it. Tack each of the top ends to a wall or two walls across a corner. Now set a large five-gallon bucket so you can tape the plastic sheeting inside the inner rim of the bucket. Fill the bucket with a several inches of soapy water. You are making a funnel of sorts with a wide open top. Wait until dark and place a small light behind the white sheeting (not behind the bucket). The insects are attracted to the light, land on the slippery plastic, slide into the bucket, and drown. You can also use this trap outdoors with a bed sheet–size piece of sheeting. Just drape the sheeting over a clothesline instead of tacking it to the wall. You might catch more than stink bugs, too.

A nuisance to gardeners, an agricultural pest to crops

Brown marmorated stink bugs, *Halyomorpha halys*, have been found in thirty-three states, including Washington, California, and Florida. The Mid-Atlantic states are taking the biggest hit, with stink bugs causing an estimated $37 million dollars of crop damage in 2010. It is an agricultural pest in its native range of China, Korea, Japan, and Taiwan. Fortunately, the stink bug is not known to harm humans.

There are hundreds of different species of stink bugs worldwide. They are easy to identify by their "shield" shape and their smell. The body of the stink bug is almost as wide as it is long, and adults reach a length of just over two thirds of an inch. The brown marmolated stink bugs are mottled brown with a distinguishing characteristic: light bands on the antennae. These insects belong to the "true bug" insect order Hemiptera, which means half wing. If you look closely you will notice that half of the insect's wing is leathery and half is clear. The 50,000 to 80,000 species of Hemipterians are really the only insects that should be called bugs out of the millions of species of other insects—to an entomologist, these are the only true bugs.

The stink bug has piercing mouthparts, much like a mosquito's. It uses its proboscis to suck juices from many of its favorite fruits and vegetables, like apples, grapes, peaches, tomatoes, green peppers, beans, squash, corn, soybeans, and other crops. The piercing of the fruit or vegetables blemishes it and makes it less marketable to fresh fruit dealers. Because of this threat to crops, the brown marmorated stink bug has attracted the notice of the US Department of Agriculture and Penn State researchers, who are working on methods to repel, lure, and eliminate the bugs from our crops. One method they are working on is finding a parasitic wasp (see page 128) that will kill the eggs of the insect.

Stink bugs, as you know if you have ever agitated one, have scent glands located on the dorsal side of the abdomen and the underside of the thorax that give off a bad odor. There is some debate whether the odor of this particular "stink bug" is unpleasant. Some say it smells like cilantro, and others like rotting food.

COCKROACHES

For most people, nothing makes the skin crawl like the sight of cockroaches scurrying around the house. No matter how clean your house is, if you see one roach, you probably have a hundred. To make matters worse, you could have more than one species of cockroach infesting your home at the same time.

Ridding your home of roaches

There are many commercial products available that target roaches, the most common of which are pesticide sprays or bait preparations. With a bit of knowledge of cockroach lifestyles and food preferences, you *can* outsmart the unstoppable roach! Most cockroaches love sweet foods. Use their sweet tooth against them to whip up Sweet Roach Bait (see page 22)—a deadly dessert. When the roach eats the bait, its body fluids will turn to water, and the gas it produces will virtually explode the insect. This is a great bait to use if you have children or pets, as it is less toxic than most baits.

Cockroaches like to run in sheltered areas (like along baseboards or above cupboards), so make some sticky traps and place them in these areas. It's easy—just place double-sided tape or spray some adhesive like picture mounting adhesive or (if the adhesive is not strong enough for the big roaches) smear Tanglefoot on one side of a four-inch-square piece of cardboard. (Tanglefoot, an extremely sticky product perfect for making traps, is available at garden supply stores.) Make several and experiment with the size. When the roaches run across the trap and get stuck, you simply wrap the trap in a piece of old newspaper and throw it into the trash or compost (assuming the roaches are dead or dying). You will need to keep children and pets away from these, especially if you use Tanglefoot, because the sticky substance is hard to remove from skin and hair.

Another trap idea is based on the fact that roaches like beer. (Who knew?) Take a large jar, at least five to six inches tall (or a coffee can) and wrap masking tape around it to the top. Then put a slice of bread soaked in beer at the bottom. The roaches climb up the tape-wrapped jar and fall into the jar of beer bread, but then they cannot climb up the slick glass or metal interior sides to get out. Dispose of them either by placing in the freezer for at least twenty-four hours to kill the roaches or by whatever means you choose.

There are a few cockroach species that prefer a less-sweet dinner. Try a sweet treat first and if you continue to see roaches, switch to a fatty bait.

Sugar is a favorite bait that both ants and roaches love. Try using a bait of equal parts boric acid (see warning, page 10) and sugar or baking soda and sugar. These baits can be used in many ways—see the ant section on page 10 for more ideas on safely using these baits.

Baits containing boric acid can be harmful when consumed over time. Care should always be taken when using any bait to make sure that children and pets can't get to it and eat it.

There are a few more interesting roach repellants that are worth trying:

- Catnip can be dried or used fresh by placing it in bowls or small sachets. Put it in cupboards or areas where roaches have been seen. Catnip made into a tea can also be wiped on counters and sprayed on baseboards to keep roaches out. Using catnip like this could drive your cat crazy, so if you have cats that are susceptible to catnip's lure (many cats are not), you should probably try something else. Bay leaves and garlic are also known to repel roaches. Bay leaves are easy to place in cupboards, but you'll need to replace them when their scent fades.

- Sprinkle boric acid (which is very inexpensive and available at most home and garden centers; see warning, page 10) under the sink, behind appliances, along garage walls, and anywhere else roaches like to hide. The roaches cross this powder, ingest it, and die. Food-grade diatomaceous earth works slightly differently: when it gets on the insects, it cuts away at their bodies so they dry out and die.

Sweet Roach Bait

1 part sugar
1 part baking soda

Combine the sugar and baking soda. Put the mixture in jar lids and place them in your kitchen and/or garage, along walls and baseboards, under sinks, or wherever you've seen roaches.

Fatty Roach Bait

$^1/_2$ cup boric acid (see warning, page 10) or borax
$^1/_8$ cup sugar
Bacon drippings
Flour

Combine the dry ingredients with enough bacon drippings to form a paste. Add some flour, if needed, to form soft balls. Place marble-size balls on wax paper wherever you see roaches, being very careful to keep it away from pets and children (the bacon makes this bait especially attractive to dogs). Discard when dry. Store extra balls in the freezer for later use.

Roaches: public enemy number one

Cockroaches are members of the Blattaria suborder of insects and are easily recognized by their flattened oval shape. In North America, there are about fifty known species. Cockroaches have been recorded on earth for 350 million years in fossil records, and some scientists speculate they will still be here long after most life on earth is gone.

Cockroaches, which arrived in the United States as stowaways, are tropical insects that prefer warm climates, but they have certainly adapted to colder ones. The roach is not known to transmit any specific disease to humans, but it is a major household pest whose nocturnal food-hunting habits have driven many a homeowner crazy. Some of the more common cockroach pests are the German cockroach, wood cockroach, Oriental cockroach, and American cockroach.

Female cockroaches reproduce using an egg capsule called an *ootheca*. The eggs are laid inside the capsule and are either carried around by the female or dropped. There can be hundreds of young roaches, which look like tiny adults, in each capsule.

You think you have a roach problem? Just imagine how much more daunting pest control would be if you had Madagascar hissing cockroaches, which are over four inches long. And this will make you feel even luckier: prehistoric roaches were over *six* inches long.

Though to many people cockroaches are simply repulsive, their survival skills are truly remarkable. Many chemicals have been developed to kill roaches, but these insects have an amazing ability to become resistant to chemicals in a very short time. Cockroaches can also live for long periods without food. Roaches have been known to survive in vacant houses for years, with only wallpaper paste for nourishment.

DUST MITES

There is a lot of advertising about having your home cleaned for dust mites, but what are these creatures? Are they really a problem?

Home invaders

People with allergies may indeed be allergic to dust mites, because you can find these tiny microscopic insects just about anywhere in your home. They like to live anywhere dust can be found, like bedding, furniture, carpets, drapes, stuffed animals, or bookcases. According to the American College of Asthma, Allergy and Immunology, approximately 10 percent of Americans exhibit allergic sensitivity to dust mites. Symptoms associated with dust mite allergies include sneezing; itchy, watery eyes; nasal stuffiness and runny nose; stuffy ears; eczema; and respiratory problems like asthma.

A typical mattress in a home with dust mites can have anywhere from one hundred thousand to ten million dust mites.

How do you know whether you have a problem with dust mites? If your allergies get worse after dusting your home, that may be the reason, but a trip to your doctor for dust mite allergy screening is the only way to know for sure.

Dust mites do not bite; they live on the dead skin cells and hair we shed. They are common in household settings, especially in bedrooms and kitchens. Dust mites can survive in all climates but prefer warm houses over 70°F, with humidity levels above 50 percent. They must have humidity to live, but they can get it from sources you may not think of—like your breath on a pillow. Areas of the country with high temperatures and humidity have a greater problem with dust mites.

Controlling dust mites

Your goal here is to control the allergen (dust mites and their feces) and also the household dust they love.

- Clean weekly. Use a damp cloth or microfiber cloth to dust everything.
- Wash bedding weekly in water at least 130°F. Lower temperatures won't kill dust mites.
- Remove all carpeting and replace with a hard flooring. This may be very important in a bedroom if the allergy is severe. If this isn't possible, have your carpet steam cleaned at least once a year.
- Never use a broom or feather duster to clean solid surfaces; that can just move dust around and not pick it up.
- Change pillows from feather fill to a synthetic fill.
- Encase your mattress in a plastic cover. When you wash your bedding, wipe down the cover.
- Drapes and blinds can be dust magnets. Install vertical or other blinds that can be vacuumed or dusted easily. Can't give up your drapes? Then find ones that can be washed regularly.
- Vacuum with a machine that has high-rated high-efficiency particulate-arresting (HEPA) filter bags or filtering system. Vacuums without HEPA filters can make the problem worse by moving the dust mites around.
- Purchase an air filter designed to remove airborne allergens. Look for ones with a HEPA filter.

- Change your heating or air conditioning filter regularly and replace it with one that traps allergens. Studies have shown that running your air conditioner in hot humid summer months can reduce dust mites by 50 percent.

- Children's plush toys can be put in the freezer for at least twenty-four hours or washed in hot water to kill dust mites.

Dust mite biology

Dust mites are extremely small and thus not visible to the naked eye. You would need at least a 10x magnification lens to see the 250- to 300-micron mite. Dust mites are not insects but true mites, more closely related to spiders. If you manage to see one, magnified, you'll notice that they have eight hairy legs, an oval-shaped translucent body, no eyes, and no antennae. The dust mite common to the United States is the American house dust mite. There is also a European house dust mite. A female dust mite lays from forty to one hundred eggs. It takes about one month for a dust mite to become an adult. Females can live from two to four months after hatching, but once the males reach adulthood they live only another ten to nineteen days.

MICE AND RATS

A rodent infestation is usually pretty obvious and often overwhelming. The first signs of a rodent most people see are the droppings they leave behind. In the garden, rats and mice will dig up seeds and generally make a mess.

A mouse in your house?

The first step in eliminating rodents from your property is to try to eliminate any food or shelter the rodents need. Sometimes your garden is the food source, so removing it isn't practical. In that case, you will have to concentrate your efforts on destroying the rodents' shelter. One way to do this is to plug any entry holes that they're using with coarse steel wool. Wait until nighttime, when the rodents are outside foraging for food, and then plug the holes. This is usually a temporary measure (because steel wool left to the elements will rust away), but it is quick and will give you time to do proper repairs. Steel wool placed around pipes indoors will keep rodents from moving from room to room.

Never leave cat or dog food outside for rodents to find. They are smarter than they look and will take advantage of this easy food source.

Mice especially love hiding under mulch that drought-conscious gardeners use to keep water loss to a minimum, so if you need to use mulch, rake it often to keep the mice from making this area their home. Be aware that rats are especially fond of ivy and similar high, dense ground covers.

Rats and mice are sensitive to certain smells. Spray outdoor baseboards with a solution of ammonia and water to deter them. Indoors, try soaking cotton balls in peppermint oil and wiping or placing them where you see rodents or evidence of rodents. They also dislike the smells of daffodils, hyacinths, and *Scilla* plants (such as bluebells). Try planting some in trouble spots.

Keeping the rodents out of your garden is much more difficult. Solid barriers around your garden will help deter most rodents, but they usually find a way around or under such barriers. Burying a $^1/_4$-inch wire mesh barrier at least six inches deep is more effective.

Rodent Bait

1 part oatmeal, cereal, or ground grain
1 part cement
Paper cups

Cut down the paper cups to about 1 inch deep. Combine the cement and oatmeal. Place the mixture in the cups and locate them where the rodents can find them but other animals can't.

Building a better mousetrap

Most people feel baiting or trapping the rodents is the only way to really make a dent in the population. Everyone is familiar with the basic snap traps, and they are still used and preferred by many people. Peanut butter makes excellent bait for a mouse snap trap. KetchAll, a new trap used by many zoos, is based on the paddle wheel principle. It resembles an old-fashioned jack-in-the-box with a hole through the base. You place the trap along a mouse path, and when the mice run through the hole, they are caught in a holding chamber. This can catch many mice (up to twenty) alive, depending on how many times you wind the trap. However, you're then faced with the unpleasant job of disposing of the live mice. It's up to you to figure out how you want to get rid of them. (Animal control won't help you, but some pest control companies will trap and take the mice away and kill them—for a fee.) If you don't want to kill the rodents, your only choice is to drive them out into the country and drop them off in a field. However, this is illegal in some areas, so check first before dumping them. An important reminder here is to check live traps daily. Failure to do this will doom the forgotten mice to suffer a slow death by starvation.

A glue board is another trap that is much less kind. The mice and rats run across it and get stuck to it. You have to decide how to kill the caught rodent and then throw the entire board away.

Poison baits are popular with some people because they are easy to use, and generally you don't have to dispose of the rodents afterward. These baits come in grain, block, and pellet forms with a variety of killing agents. They are used with tamper-resistant bait stations or boxes that prevent pets or other animals from eating the bait. You can make your own homemade oatmeal-cement bait (see page 26), which is very effective—the rodents die because they can't digest the cement. When using poison baits, always be look on the label to make sure it states "No secondary kill." This means if a hawk or other predator finds a dying rodent and eats it, it won't kill the predator too.

Sound devices to repel rodents seem like a great solution, but many people have limited success with them. It's true that mice don't like the noises these produce, but they will get used to them. If you have a problem in a small space, then this might be worth a try.

A battery-run high-tech device that stuns mice and rats to death is the "Rat Zapper." It uses batteries and stuns the rodents like a stun gun and kills them quickly. It is best used indoors but can be used outdoors if covered in plastic or protected from the elements. It kills only one rodent at a time. Then the rodent must be removed and the trap reset.

When handling rodents (dead or alive), always wear rubber or plastic gloves that can be washed with a bleach and water mixture, and place dead rodents in sealed double plastic bags before placing in the trash.

A rodent's world

Rats and mice are able to live in a variety of environments, and no place is safe from these invaders. Any crevice with access wider than one-quarter inch can be a perfect home. Some of their favorite places are sewers, basements, stables, and burrows under rocks and buildings. Every zoo in the world has an ongoing fight with rodents. The lure of free food and lodging is just too much for the rodents to resist.

Rats and mice are very prolific. Mice start breeding at about eight weeks of age and rats at about three months. Each can have a litter four times a year, averaging eight to nine young per litter. Rodents cause major economic damage and can transmit infectious diseases such as plague and typhus to humans.

Most rats and mice are nocturnal and have favorite runs and paths along sides of buildings, baseboards, and fences. They also have excellent senses of hearing, taste, and smell; eyesight is their weakest sense.

TERMITES

No other insects brings terror to the hearts of homeowners like termites. These small insects can skeletonize the wood in your home until it is barely standing. Repairs are usually costly and inconvenient. But how do you figure out whether you have the little home wreckers—before it's too late?

Looking for the silent destroyers

Most people don't realize that they have termites until it's too late and they're looking at large repair bills. Just a little snooping can save your wallet and your house.

Start in your garage, which is generally the first place dry-wood termite signs will be noticed. Once a month, look around the floor of your garage for a sand-like substance. It is about the size of onion seeds or cracked pepper and is generally a mixture of rust and cream colors. If you have a small magnifying glass, look at this substance to see if each granule has six long grooves. This substance, called *frass*, is excreted by the termite and pushed out of an exit hole in the wood. The grooves are formed when the excrement passes from the termite's body.

If you find frass, look directly up for the exit hole, which will look like a nail hole. There may be one or more of them. You now have a place to start fighting the little creatures.

Be sure to check wooden patio covers and decks this way also. Outdoors, winds can blow away the frass quickly, so try the following trick: hold a sheet of white paper under the section you want to check, and tap the wood with a rubber mallet or small hammer. You'll be able to see the frass as it falls onto the paper. Check carefully around corners and seams, which are termites' favorite places to enter the wood. Don't think you're safe because you have a redwood patio or deck—termites will attack redwood, also.

If your house has a raised foundation, you'll need to get out your trusty flashlight to check for subterranean termites. These termites construct earthen tubes from the soil to the wood in your home. Check for these tubes along the inside and outside of your home's foundation. Also look for mud coming out between boards or along the foundation. A knife blade poked along your foundation or supporting studs will easily pierce an affected board. Extremely tunneled boards will sound hollow when tapped with a hammer.

Treatment options

Now that you've found the pests, it's time to figure out what kinds of treatments are available to you as a homeowner, and especially which treatments you can do yourself.

First, try to determine how extensive your infestation is. Is only one board infested? Is it easy to get to? If there are more boards affected, do they show signs of weakness? Tap boards and watch for falling frass, look for exit holes, and check for the most serious sign: very hollow-sounding boards with easily exposed tunnels. Remember that termites chew through wood slowly, so finding evidence of their existence doesn't mean they will devour your home in a week. You have plenty of time to plan your attack.

If you don't trust yourself to determine how extensive your problem is, call one of the many termite companies that offer a free home inspection. Watching the inspector work will also help you do the job again yourself. Ask the inspector to show you what frass or earthen tubes look like, and, if frass is found, keep some for later comparison.

The diagnosis of termites used to mean all-out chemical pesticide warfare against the insects. Some pesticides that were used routinely had a residual effect of up to twenty-five years. Luckily, homeowners today have numerous options, many of which do not rely on any pesticides.

One of the most effective methods of control for drywood termites is to just remove and replace infected boards. Often this is the easiest and cheapest method. When you remove a board, check the ends of the board carefully to see whether the termites have tunneled out of that board into the next. If no exit tunnels are found, your problem may be solved.

Termite companies have many nonchemical weapons in their arsenal against termites, including microwave radiation, electricity, orange oil, heat, and cold. Specially designed equipment shoots the radiation, electricity, or orange oil directly into the termites' nest, killing them. Another machine can heat wood to over 150°F, which kills the insects. Still another machine freezes the wood, destroying the termites. The amount and area of wood that needs to be treated and the conditions where you live may determine which of these methods would be perfect for your situation.

Pesticides *are* still used to combat termites because several pesticide fumigates are very effective against this particular pest. Fumigation treatments have been popular because the entire house can be treated at once, they can kill termites that live in hard to reach areas of a home, or they are required for certification when buying or selling a home. A few products can be purchased by the homeowner, but many can only be obtained by professional termite exterminators. Unless you know exactly how to effectively spray for termites, it is best to leave large-area treatment to the professionals.

When only a few boards need to be treated, you can use a spot spray (labeled for use against ants and termites) that comes with a long flexible tube. Place the end of the tube over a termite exit hole, then start spraying until you see spray backing up into the tube or coming out another exit hole. Go to the next exit hole and spray again, continuing until no further exit holes are found. This spray works well on drywood and powder-post termites, because they are usually confined. You'll want to keep an eye on the treated area to make sure frass doesn't start appearing again.

If you discover you have subterranean termites, the earthen tube must be destroyed before treatment can begin. With these termites, both the wood and the soil must be treated. Subterranean termites eat your wood but always maintain some contact with the soil. Breaking this contact is essential for complete control over this type of termite.

Finally, if all else fails or the area to be treated is very large, the only option left may be to have your entire house fumigated. The good thing about this method is that it will also kill any roaches or ants that have made their home in your home. The bad news is that it kills any beneficial spiders in your home as well.

chapter three

Garden Pest Control

ANTS IN THE GARDEN

You may be distressed to find that the same little critters that have been plaguing you in your home are in your garden as well. It seems like they're everywhere, and they are—except the polar regions. What to do (besides move to Antarctica)?

Attacking the ant army

Because many species of ants look alike, you could have many different species living in your home and yard at the same time without even realizing it. Knowing what type of food the ants are after will help you determine what control method will work best. If ants attack your fruit trees, try the Chile-Vinegar Spray on page 35. (**Warning:** Some solutions—especially those containing oils and soaps—can burn delicate plants, causing the leaves to dry up and fall off. Before you use any new solution on a plant, test it first on one or two leaves. If those leaves still look healthy after a day or two, go ahead and do a full treatment.)

For ants elsewhere in the garden, try Ant Death Bait (see page 35), served in a jar lid or cut-down paper cup. Place the cups throughout your garden and yard where you know ants will find them. To protect dogs and other animals from getting into the cups, it may be necessary to cover the cup with a cardboard box (weighed down with a heavy rock). Poke small holes into the base of the box with an ice pick to give ants easy access but keep pets from eating the poison. **Warning:** Please note that boric acid is a liver and kidney toxin which, over time, can cause sickness in children and pets. A small one-time dose will most likely cause only an upset stomach; however, in the case of more severe ingestion, contact the poison control center in your area.

Fire ants

If you have these in your garden, you need to act now. Fire ants are small aggressive ants that were accidentally introduced into the United States from South America. The black fire ant was introduced in the late teens or early 1920s, and the red fire ant (now called the red imported fire ant or RIFA) in the 1930s. Fire ants have been spreading since their introduction and are established in southeastern states including Texas. Several other states have isolated areas with fire ants. The sting of the fire ant creates severe pain, a red welt, and, for some people, allergic reactions. These ants can overwhelm and kill small animals and birds, and they are known to be destructive to some agricultural commodities. Their mounds can be seen dotting farm and pasture lands. The underground nesting system can reach three feet deep.

Getting rid of the ants

Eliminating fire ants can be a big job, and using only nontoxic methods may not be enough. Your goal is to kill the queen, but she can be deep in the mound and hard to get to. An IPM (integrated pest management) system may be needed. This system uses cultural, mechanical, nontoxic, and, if necessary, spot low-toxicity pesticide treatments to control a pest. If you decide to use anything that is not nontoxic, read the label carefully, especially if it is to be used in or near a garden.

So, you say, what can I do? The ant eradication ideas and recipes in chapter 2 (see page 10) will work on ants, including fire ants, but here are a few more ideas:

- Ring the mound with food-grade diatomaceous earth (see warning, page 12). Ants won't cross it, and you cut off their food supply. Then put a bait treatment inside the ring. They have no choice but to eat the bait. Reapply after rain.
- Look for new, less toxic fire ant control products. One has an orange citrus base; the other uses spinosad, derived from a bacterium that kills only insects.
- Some people claim that powdered cinnamon poured down the mound works.
- Pour a soapy solution in the mound. This will kill some but probably not all of the ants. Soapy water poured around your house foundation is reported to keep ants out of your house, too.
- Talcum powder is reported to repel the ants.
- Pour boric acid (see warning, page 10) directly into the mound; you can also use it around foundations to keep the ants out. A good product is "Hot Shot Roach Powder," which is almost 100-percent boric acid. It is inexpensive and available at most garden centers.

If you are going to treat fire ants, it is best to do it early in the morning when the ants are less active. Also, if you are going to apply a solution directly to the mound or the surrounding soil, it will be more effective if the soil is already damp. This will allow for better absorption of the solution.

Ants: soil workers

Ants, as bothersome as they can be to people, do serve a function in nature. Besides being scavengers, ants are great soil mixers. Ants turn over tons of dirt building their nests, and they are often called the composters of the insect world.

Besides working the soil, ants are scrupulously clean. They have a comb on the middle joint of each front leg they use to clean their bodies. Some birds will actually allow ants to crawl on their bodies to clean them of unwanted parasites.

When ants die, their fellow ants carry off the bodies to an ant morgue. Although to humans this looks like a very difficult task, ants can lift fifty times their body weight without effort.

Chile-Vinegar Spray for Fruit Trees

4 jalapeño, habanero, or other hot chiles, seeded and chopped
2 cloves garlic
1¹/₂ quarts water
2 ounces beer (try using the rest of the bottle or can as
    snail bait)
¹/₂ cup vinegar

Combine the peppers, garlic, water, and beer in a saucepan.
Cover and bring to a boil for 5 minutes, then let the mixture steep
in the pot for 24 hours. Add the vinegar, strain well, and pour into
a sprayer. Discard the strained solids. Test a leaf first for burning before spraying the entire tree. Spray the leaves only, not the
blossoms.

Ant Death Bait

1 tablespoon boric acid powder (see warning, page 10)
1 tablespoon white sugar
¹/₃ cup water

Combine the boric acid powder, sugar, and water. Divide between
two small jar lids or cut-down paper cups. Place where you see ants.

 # APHIDS

A lone aphid doesn't look very threatening, but in
numbers they can suck the life out of your flowers
and garden vegetables. They can deform the leaves of your favorite ornamental shrub, and the sticky "honeydew" they secrete will draw ants
from nearby nests.

Help is on the way: aphid predators

Luckily for you, there are many naturally occurring aphid predators. The best known of these is the ladybird beetle or ladybug. Both the larval form and the adults prey on aphids. Other aphid predators include lacewings, syrphid fly larvae, and wasps. The adult forms of many of these predators eat only nectar and pollen, so you can encourage them by planting nectar-rich flowers and plants that produce a lot of pollen in and around your garden. Some good choices are daisies, mint, carrots, anise, and chives.

To stop a small infestation of aphids, a simple trimming or a strong spraying from the hose will sometimes do the trick. If somewhat stronger methods are needed, try one of the following.

To protect a desired vegetable, a sacrificial vegetable can be planted. If you know that the aphids in your garden love cabbage (and they usually do), plant some! The aphids will go for the cabbage and leave your other vegetables alone. This also makes the "seek and destroy" method of killing aphids much easier because they will be congregated in one spot.

It has been calculated that in 2.5 acres of crops there could be as many as five *trillion* aphids, which could produce two tons of honeydew a day.

However, if you want to grow cabbage and not give it to the aphids, try planting yellow and orange nasturtiums; these will also attract the pesky aphids. They can make an excellent garden border or companion planting. (Unfortunately, the nasturtiums may not look great with the aphids attacking them.) Nasturtiums planted around apple trees also work well at drawing the always unwanted woolly aphid away from the tree. One caution about planting nasturtiums is that in temperate regions they can become invasive. If this could be a problem in your area, plant the nasturtiums in pots and place them where needed.

If you find that aphids are attacking your roses, mulch banana peels into the soil at the base of the rose bushes. This will strengthen the roses to ward off disease-bearing aphids.

Try spraying your plants with a mild soap solution (one tablespoon of soap dissolved in a gallon of water), but keep in mind that some plants are easily burned by soap—especially those with fuzzy leaves. Try your soap solution on a few leaves first and check them for burning after one hour if they are in direct sun and then again in twenty-four hours. If you notice any burning, don't use a soap product or rinse the soap off after a few minutes following the treatment.

The new insecticidal soaps now available at garden supply stores kill aphids using fatty acids. They are very effective but must be used carefully and according to package directions.

Controlling the ants in your yard and garden can greatly reduce the aphid population (see page 32). Equal parts boric acid (see warning, page 10) and sugar sprinkled in your garden will help. For complete recipes and more ant tips, see pages 32–35.

Aphids are attracted to anything yellow. Buy yellow sticky traps and place them on a wooden stake or fence in your garden. Farmers and nurseries also use these traps to identify other yellow-loving insects that may be present. This is actually a good way to get to know which common insects, both good and bad, are visiting your garden. Make your own traps out of yellow plastic plates and spray cooking oil like Pam. Spray the cooking oil fairly heavily on the plate and place the traps in and around your garden. Check your trap regularly; when it is dirty or full of aphids and other critters, wipe it clean and start over again. A yellow plastic bucket filled with water and a bit of liquid soap will also work.

Aluminum foil and reflective plastic mulches are known to repel aphids from summer squashes, melons, and other vegetables. The aluminum foil mulch comes in rolls and is used to cover the row before planting. Following the spacing recommendations on seed packets or seedling (start) packs, cut three- to four-inch holes for the plants in the mulch. Plant as usual. Reflective plastic mulches, available in garden stores, can be placed around the seedlings. You can also make your own by spraying clear plastic with silver paint. In areas where it gets hot in the summer, to prevent burning, remove the mulch before the day gets hot. A benefit of reflective mulches is generally a greater vegetable yield.

Commercially available insect growth regulators (IGRs) are artificial insect growth hormones that are sprayed on plants to target specific insect pests, such as aphids. They work by interfering with the insect's growth, development, or reproduction, stopping the life cycle of the pest. Many people are already familiar with IGRs in the new flea-treatment products, and these regulators are sure to increase in popularity as people become more aware of them. Ask for them at your local nursery.

Know your plant-sucking enemy

Aphids are one of the most economically destructive insects. They not only destroy crops and plants, but the money spent on pesticides to control them is astronomical.

Aphids, which are also called plant lice, are pear-shaped insects that suck the juices out of plant leaves, roots, and stems. They are characterized by two tube-like structures (cornicles) rising from the back of the abdomen. Aphids come in various sizes, but most are $1/16$ to $1/8$ inch long. They are usually some shade of green, but there are also brown, yellow, pink, and black species.

Aphids have a complex life cycle. One of the most interesting aspects is that almost all the aphids you see in your yard are female. They reproduce without the need for male aphids and produce only wingless female offspring. This process, called *parthenogenesis*, goes on for several generations. Males and females with wings are produced only when it is time to lay eggs that need to overwinter.

Aphids produce honeydew, a sweet, sticky substance that ants love to eat. It has been determined that ants will actually tend the honeydew-producing aphids called *ant cows*. Not only will the ants harvest the honeydew for food, but they will protect and defend the aphids as well. Some species of aphids have become so dependent on the care of ants that without them they couldn't survive. A good example of this interdependence is the corn root aphid, which depends on ants to carry it from one corn root to another as the need arises. Here is where controlling ants in your yard or garden can greatly reduce the aphid population.

Honeydew that dries on the plant appears shiny and can cause problems for a plant by becoming the medium for mold. Black mold, which has long been associated with aphids, can coat leaves and reduce the plant's photosynthesis abilities. The aphid's role as a vector of disease is another major threat to plants. Just as the mosquito carries malaria from person to person, the winged form of the aphid carries diseases from plant to plant.

CABBAGE LOOPERS

Let's say all the plants in your garden look good, except the plants in the cabbage family (cole crops). The leaves have ragged holes, and you've found caterpillars moving like inch worms. Most likely those are cabbage loopers feeding on your prized cabbages.

Throwing loopers for a loop

Every state in North America has some form of cabbage looper. Cabbage loopers are the caterpillars of several species of moths, and many people have no idea that their caterpillar forms are pests. The loopers feed on a variety of plants and flowers, but they really love cabbage, broccoli, brussels sprouts, collards, cauliflower, kale, mustard, radish, rutabaga, turnip, and watercress. Other vegetable crops that they can injure include beet, canta-loupe, celery, cucumber, lima bean, lettuce, parsnip, pea, pepper, potato, snap bean, spinach, squash, sweet potato, tomato, and watermelon. The loopers will also bore into developing heads of the plants. So there goes your cabbage crop. What can you do?

Place lightweight row covers over your developing plants in early spring when the adult moths are looking for susceptible plants on which to lay their eggs. There is a commercial pheromone trap available if your prob-lem is severe. The traps will attract the adults and help you determine when to take action. Many gardeners just recommend keeping the row covers in place all season. You can water through them, and the covers give the plants some protection from frost for a longer growing season.

If you have a minor problem with loopers, handpicking them off as you find them always works well. Encouraging natural enemies may also be enough control. Start by planting parsley, dill, fennel, coriander, and alys-sum on the borders of your garden. These plants have flowers that attract many beneficial insects. *Trichogramma* wasps, for example, destroy looper eggs by laying their own eggs in them.

Another approach to halting the looper invasion is to apply *Bacillus thuringiensis* (Bt), on the leaves of your plants at the first sign of loopers or when the plants are small. Bt works very well on small caterpillars. The loopers must eat the Bt, which will leave some damage, but the loopers will die quickly. Reapply if necessary as the plant grows, following label directions.

Be sure to pull up susceptible crops after the last harvest and dispose of plants to kill any cocoons attached to plants. Clean up any garden plant debris promptly after the growing season to keep down looper numbers.

A looper lifestyle

The cabbage looper, *Trichoplusia ni*, is a member of the night-flying Noctuidae moth family. Moths emerge in spring and females can lay between three hundred and six hundred eggs on host plants. The young caterpillars (loopers) hatch out in three to four days. The loopers are primarily green, have three sets of small legs, and some have a white stripe running along each side of their bodies. Loopers got their name from the way they move, much like inchworms (Geometridae), arching their backs by pulling the back half of the body in and moving forward by projecting the front half of the body, but they are not related to inchworms. The looper will reach an average length of $1^{1}/_{2}$ inches and mature in two to four weeks from hatching. The looper then forms a cocoon attached to the underside of a leaf, on a stem, or in plant debris. The adult emerges in about ten days as a dull gray moth with a wingspan of $1^{1}/_{2}$ inches. Cabbage loopers can produce many generations in a single year.

CORN EARWORMS

You know the damage. Tips of corn ears that have been eaten away—or worse, the earworm caterpillar is still there, chewing away under the husk. Leaves may appear to be peppered with buckshot, or the stalks may have sawdust-filled holes caused by the earworms boring. Is there anything that will really work to save your sweet corn?

The key: protection and perseverance

The adult corn earworm, a moth that is a common pest of corn, will also feed on tomatoes, potatoes, and peppers. It will deposit its eggs on the corn silks or on the underside of leaves. Your goal is to prevent the earworm caterpillar from reaching the ear of corn and causing damage to your crop. Once the corn earworm is inside the ear of corn, eradication is difficult.

Because this pest has been around a long time, it has many natural enemies—such as lacewings, minute pirate bugs, and damsel bugs—that feed on the eggs and caterpillars. The *Trichogramma* wasp will lay its eggs in the eggs of the earworm. These eggs turn black and are easily identified. Don't destroy these black eggs; the wasp larva inside will mature and hatch into more wasps, ready to seek out more corn earworm eggs. Biological controls like these insects take time, and some damage is expected. Some of these biological control insects can be purchased (see the Resources and Buying Guide section of this book) and released early in the season before the moth populations are high.

Pair these good bugs with a few natural controls for better protection. The old trick of putting oil on the silks works by preventing the earworm from reaching the corn ear. There are lots of recipes for when to apply it and how much oil to use. There are two common recipes: (1) place twenty drops of mineral oil on the tip of each ear when silks appear; (2) place five drops of mineral oil or corn oil on corn ear tips when the silks begin to turn brown. Both oil applications are only done once.

If the corn earworm was a big problem for you last season, try treating emerging ears and leaves with Bt when the silk has partially emerged. If you live in an area with a long growing season, try planting your sweet corn early, before the moths are numerous. When harvesting is completed, remove and dispose of old stalks quickly to kill any late earworms.

A corn earworm's life

The corn earworm moth, *Heliothis zea*, is a widespread pest that is most active during the evening and night. The adults are approximately $3/4$ of an inch long with a wingspan of $1/2$ to 1 inch. Moth coloration varies, from tan to olive green to dark reddish brown. The adult moths will lay eggs throughout the corn growing season, but their populations are highest during August and September. The female moth will deposit one tiny white egg on the leaves or on their favorite spot, fresh corn silk. The young earworm will hatch in five to seven days; it is greenish with a black head. The earworm feeds on the silk on its way to the corn ear tip. A fully mature earworm will reach a length of $1^{1}/_{2}$ inches in two to four weeks, and at that time it will emerge from the plant and fall to the ground, where it pupates in the soil. Adults can emerge in ten to twenty-five days, and there can be up to four generations per year.

CUCUMBER BEETLES

The leaves of your beautiful garden of cucumbers, melons, squashes, beans, peas, corn, beets, tomatoes, and potatoes are suddenly full of small holes. To make matters worse, now you are finding holes in some of your prized tree fruit and in flowers such as daisies and cosmos. Is it possible that the $^{1}/_{4}$- to $^{1}/_{3}$-inch beetles you're finding on the underside of leaves are doing all this damage? You bet!

Controlling cucumber beetles

In large corn plantings, farmers plow under all the old corn plants to deprive this hard-to-control beetle of shelter and thereby keep its numbers down. This is something all gardeners can do when each planting is finished producing. By removing all dead and finished plants and discarding or composting them, you remove the shelter needed by the adults to overwinter.

Planting early and late in the season can also help you avoid the beetles' peak season—the summer. Another technique is to place a fine screen or small milk cartons over young seedlings. The beetles can destroy seedlings quickly, but most plants can tolerate the beetles' feeding once they're past the seedling stage.

Interplanting with such beetle-repellent plants as catnip, tansy, geraniums, and marigolds is known to help discourage the beetles. Radishes and nasturtiums are especially helpful. Make beetle traps from open cans or milk cartons baited with garden targets, especially pieces of melon. Place these traps around your garden and check them early in the morning. (If you wait too long, the beetles will eat all the bait and leave before you have a chance to destroy them.)

If you have a strong stomach and a spare old blender, you can also use the trap-caught beetles to prepare Cucumber Beetle Death Repellent. Beetles don't like the smell of dead beetles in their feeding area, so this mixture should keep them away.

Cucumber Beetle Death Repellent

50 (or more) cucumber beetles
2 cups water

Kill the beetles by placing them in a jar with a cotton ball soaked in fingernail polish remover or in the freezer. Put the dead beetles in a blender with the water and puree. Spray or drip the mixture, which should be fairly thin, around the plants in your garden.

Strength in numbers

The cucumber beetle has long been a garden pest, found on more than two hundred kinds of weeds, grasses, and cultivated plants. This name is actually used for two beetles. The striped form (*Acalymma vittatum*) is yellow with three black stripes and a black head, and the spotted form (*Diabrotica undecimpunctata howardi* and a related Western species, *Diabrotica undecimpunctata undecimpunctata*) are greenish yellow with twelve black spots and a black head. The spotted cucumber beetle is also known by another name— corn rootworm—that describes the damage it does.

Both species have the same life cycle. The adults like to hibernate and spend the winter in old garden debris and around the bases of old plants. The adults emerge in early spring and lay their eggs at the base of host plants. After the eggs hatch, the larvae burrow into the soil, looking for tender roots and underground parts of the stem. Here they can cause a lot of damage to gardens and crops, especially corn. The larvae continue to cause root damage until summer, when they pupate and emerge as new adults in July. Then the adults do their damage by chewing holes in the plant and transmitting viral and bacterial wilt diseases.

Very little is known about the natural predators of the cucumber beetle. There are a few natural predators, including tachinid flies, but they have little effect on the beetle population.

CUTWORMS

Your seedlings are looking great; then suddenly one morning you find them lying on the ground. Check for chewing at the base of the plant or on its roots, because the problem could be cutworms.

Cutting the worms off

Cutworms are the larvae or caterpillars of several species of moths in the Noctuidae family. They eat a wide variety of plants, but they really love young plants, particularly in the cabbage family, as well as plants such as tomatoes, carrots, corn, beans, peppers, and squash. There are also cutworms that eat turf grass. Because the word "cutworm" is a general term for several species of caterpillars, each species may attack your plants differently. All cutworms chew, but some prefer chewing the stems at the soil, others will climb the stem to feed on leaves and buds, and still others feed underground on roots. If you have these insects, act quickly to limit the damage they can cause. Try one of the following:

- Mix one gallon water with three tablespoons dishwashing liquid. Pour on the troubled area. The soap will bring the worms to the surface, where you can either let the birds eat them or dispose of them yourself.
- Lay wooden boards next to seedlings. The cutworms will take shelter under these boards during the day. Check under the boards and dispose of the worms.

- Wrap stems of transplants and seedlings with stiff paper, toothpicks surrounding the stem held on with a twist tie, cardboard, or aluminum foil sleeves. For transplants, bury the sleeve in the soil to thwart the cutworms.

- Check plants at night when cutworms are active and collect any you see. This could be a great game for children.

- Place food-grade diatomaceous earth (see warning, page 12) next to stems and mix some around the plant.

- Carefully cultivate around the seedlings to look for any cutworms. They like to lie close to the plant just under the soil surface during the day.

- Plant older transplants. They can withstand more damage to their stems than younger seedlings.

- Sprinkle the soil around seedlings with *Bacillus thuringiensis* (Bt). This bacterium will kill the larvae of moths when it is ingested.

- Keep planting beds and paths free of weeds. Weeds can harbor the pests after crops are harvested and increase their numbers.

Cutworms are not true worms

Cutworms are really insects. When these caterpillars grow up, they will become dark gray, brown, or black night-flying moths. The adult moth's wingspan averages $1^1/_2$ inches, and different species have various wing markings. The female may lay hundreds of eggs in clusters or singly on stems and leaves of plants. They have been known to lay eggs on weeds and other plant debris.

When they emerge, the young cutworms will feed on plants and roots. They can vary in color from cream to yellowish green, brown, and black, and some have longitudinal stripes. The cutworms can reach two inches in length, and it is this larval stage that causes all the damage. When disturbed, the cutworm forms a distinctive "C" shape.

Cutworm species may have as many as four generations per year. Many cutworms will overwinter in this larval form in weedy or grassy areas. Controlling weeds is important in many areas where cutworms are a problem.

EARWIGS

Perhaps you've noticed bite marks on your flowers and the leaves of your beans, beets, corn, lettuce, strawberries, dahlias, or zinnias. On further inspection, you discover an earwig: a strange-looking insect with pincers on the end of its abdomen. These insects like to hide in dark places, but once you've found them you can stop the damage with a few simple strategies.

Bye-bye, earwig

In general, the earwig's natural predators (ants and yellow jacket wasps) do a pretty good job of keeping them in check. There is also a parasitic fly, *Digonichaeta setipennis*, that is a natural enemy of earwigs—you can encourage them to visit your yard by planting composite flowering plants; these flies also feed on buckwheat, anise, cosmos, dill, and tansy. If you notice a lot of damage, it may be wise to import another predator. The tachinid fly *Bigonicheta spinipennis* would be a good choice. This fly also likes composite flowers and planting them near your earwig problem areas will help keep them close.

Traps are another very effective control method for earwigs. Several different methods rely on the same principle. Earwigs love to hide in dry, dark places, so place rolled-up newspapers in your garden before dark. Discard the newspapers the next day, while the earwigs are still hiding in them. A six-inch piece of an old garden hose, either laid down in the garden or stuck into the ground, also makes an excellent trap. Empty the traps each morning by shaking the earwigs from the hose pieces into a bucket of soapy water.

Bait traps are also very good for catching earwigs. Bury a small can flush with the ground and fill it partially with beer. Earwigs that are attracted to the beer will fall into the can and drown. This trap also catches snails, so if you have both pests, this is the trap for you.

You can protect your garden by spraying plants with a great earwig repellent made of garlic and soap (see page 47). (It works on other unwanted insects as well.) Spot check for burning on any plant in your garden before doing a full treatment on it.

Boric acid (see warning, page 10) baits are also very effective for earwigs. Try the same one we recommend for ants (see Ant Death Bait, page 35).

Ear dwellers?

Earwigs are found throughout the United States and are easily spotted because of their large pincers. They are brown and about $^1/_2$ to $^3/_4$ inch long, with a long segmented abdomen. They belong to the insect order Dermaptera (which describes their short leathery forewings), of which eighteen species are known to exist in the United States. The earwig probably got its name from people who feared that an ear was as good a place as any for this dark-dwelling creature to live. Even today, while we *know* earwigs don't live in ears, there are a few mysterious reports each year of people rushing to emergency rooms to have these creatures removed from their ears.

Most earwig species are nocturnal scavengers that feed on decaying plant matter, but the European earwig (*Forficula auricularia*) is a greenhouse pest. Some species are very beneficial and prey on aphids and small insect larvae. Garden damage due to earwigs is usually minimal.

The earwig overwinters in pairs. A male and female will hibernate together in cells in the soil or a hollowed-out depression under an object. In the spring, the female lays her eggs and tends them until they hatch and leave the cell. Without careful cleaning of the eggs by the female, most eggs will become infected with fungus and fail to hatch. The earwig female is known as one of the truly attentive mothers of the insect world.

Earwig Repellent

5 cloves garlic
1 quart water, divided
3 drops liquid soap or detergent

Puree the garlic and 1 cup water in a blender until liquefied.

Strain the mixture and add 3 drops of soap. Add enough of the remaining water to bring the mixture to one quart. Spray on plants.

FRUIT FLIES

You cut into a big juicy piece of fruit and find small white worms crawling inside. After checking more fruit from your trees, you discover that much of the fruit has worms, and small golden flies seem to be hanging around your tree. This could be a *serious* problem.

An agricultural nightmare

In many states, fruit flies such as the Oriental fruit fly, Mexican fruit fly, melon fly, and Mediterranean fruit fly are categorized as "serious pests," requiring immediate intervention from state and/or county agricultural personnel. This usually involves the immediate sampling and surveying of fruit from host trees in the area to determine the infestation's severity. If the infestation is quite severe, it may be necessary to strip all the fruit from the infected trees. Finally, pesticide-laced bait may be sprayed on the host plants to kill any remaining flies.

Agricultural officials also have a "sterile insect" technique in their arsenal to combat these detrimental flies. This procedure releases thousands of sterile flies in an affected area. Fruit flies usually mate once, and if the ratio of sterile flies is very high, the chances of a nonsterile fly (called a *wild fly*) mating with a sterile fly will be good. You can tell a sterile fly from a nonsterile fly with a UV light. Sterile flies have a dye incorporated into their bodies during rearing. This dye will become visible under UV light. If you think you have a species of fruit fly infesting your fruit trees, call your local agricultural department for advice and an inspection.

However, it should be noted there are many kinds of fruit flies that are pests to gardeners but do not demand drastic action from agriculture officials. The cherry fruit fly is one example.

New bacterium to the rescue?

Many methods have been tried to control fruit flies, but most are marginally helpful at best. Basically you need to control them in the adult and pupal stages, because once the eggs are laid inside the fruit, it is difficult (or even impossible) to control the larvae without destroying the fruit.

Spinosad is a chemical class of insecticides that is registered to control a variety of insects. It can be found in several products on the market that homeowners can buy, and has proven to be very effective at controlling fruit flies like olive fruit fly, walnut husk fly, apple maggot, and other pests. The active ingredient spinosad is a combination of the two fermentation factors called spinosyns A and D, which are produced from a naturally occurring soil dwelling bacterium called *Saccharopolyspora spinosa*. Organic growers may only use products that are certified organic by OMRI, the Organic Material Review Institute, and many products containing spinosad have this certification. Products containing spinosad can be applied by foliar spraying or by bait application. The bait product is a mixture of spinosad and sweet bait. The bait is applied by spraying a spot on the tree or plant; the flies are attracted to the bait, eat it, and die.

Another method of fighting fruit flies is to place sticky traps among the branches of trees. Put them out in early summer, when fruits are just starting to grow. You can purchase fruit fly traps from your local nursery or make your own by spraying picture spray mount on six-by-eight-inch pieces of yellow poster board. Some commercial traps contain a fly attractant that will make them much more effective.

The adult fruit fly, like the common house fly, has only spongy mouth parts, so it can't chew on your plants. You can use this knowledge against it by spraying a boric acid (see warning, page 10) and sugar solution on your trees. The adult fly will be drawn to the sugar water on the leaves and get a lethal dose of boric acid in the process. Use the Ant Death Bait recipe on page 35—just make sure to test a few leaves for burning first. This spray will also kill ants on the infested tree. This method works best when the plant is still wet, so early morning spraying is best. However, if your tree is prone to mold, use this spray only occasionally or wash it off after a few days.

Encourage predators by planting flowers that produce a lot of pollen (like daisies) around your trees. Many adult wasps eat pollen, and they will use the fruit flies to continue their life cycle by parasitizing the fly larvae. The wasps lay their eggs on the fly larvae, and when the wasps hatch, they feed on the immature fly larvae, killing them.

The very tiny fruit flies that we've all seen hovering around ripe fruit are different from the Mediterranean fruit fly and its close relatives. The confusion arises because they are also called fruit flies, but they have other names, like vinegar fly or *Drosophila* (their scientific genus name). They can be controlled pretty easily in a small garden. Just take a hand-held vacuum cleaner out to the garden and suck them right out of the air. If they are a pest of your fruit bowl or compost crock, the vacuum works well here, too. You can also put a small bowl of apple cider vinegar on the counter; they will be attracted to it and drown. Another clever method is to put grape juice and a section of banana peel in a plastic container and enclose it in an upside-down resealable plastic bag. Snip off the two corners of the bag opposite the resealable edge and push the snipped corners inward so flies can fly in but they can't fly out.

The life of a fruit fly

All fruit flies have a similar life cycle. The adults, which resemble small, light brown houseflies with light and dark markings on their wings, lay their eggs inside developing fruit. One female may produce eight hundred eggs in her lifetime. The eggs hatch, and the white maggots, which grow to about $1/3$ inch in length, feed inside the fruit. When the larvae are full-sized, they will leave the fruit and drop to the ground to pupate. The flies will stay in the pupal form in cool areas throughout the winter; the adults emerge the following spring. However, in warm climates many generations of fruit flies can be produced throughout the year.

GRASSHOPPERS

You know them on sight. Grasshoppers! Usually they don't cause much damage, but some years the damage is worse, and they will eat anything. Is there anything that you can do before it is too late?

A moving target

There are about thirty species of grasshoppers that are garden pests in North America. It is estimated that grasshoppers eat 25 percent of the forage crops in the western half of the nation each year, causing millions of dollars of damage. Grasshoppers are hard to control because they are migratory. They are here one day and can be gone the next, leaving damage behind. Before the first sign of grasshopper feeding—the jagged holes and chewing on the edges of leaves—it's time to take action.

Fabric row covers can prevent young grasshoppers from reaching your plants, but use a weight that's substantial; grasshoppers can chew through very lightweight fabric. Some gardeners have resorted to using tougher screening material to thwart grasshoppers. Watch for grasshoppers and pick them off the cover early in the morning, when temperatures are cool and they can't move quickly. Be sure your row covers reach the ground, and anchor them with dirt or rocks to prevent the grasshoppers from getting under them.

Gardeners that live by pastures or forage crops will have a hard time battling grasshoppers because a constant supply of the insects is always near. Try growing a trap crop between the pasture and your garden. Grasshoppers like zinnias, so planting a row may help deter the pesky critters from your prized vegetables. It is also said that grasshoppers are repelled by cilantro. Grow cilantro plants around your garden, and in addition to using the leaves for salad greens and seasoning, you can harvest the seeds for your own coriander.

If grasshoppers were a big problem for you last year, plant vegetables that grasshoppers are known to dislike. Try planting peas, spinach, lettuce, and broccoli. Female grasshoppers like to lay their eggs in corn and dry-bean crops.

If you expect trouble from grasshoppers, you can apply an organic bait early in the season. Two such baits are Nolo Bait and Semaspore Grasshopper Control, which contain the spores of *Nosema locustae*. These fungal spores are mixed with bran or wheat, and the grasshoppers become infected when they eat the bait. The disease is slow-acting and will spread to other grasshoppers through cannibalism. The product is harmless to pets and people, but as with any pest control product, always follow the package directions.

Another new product for grasshopper control is kaolin clay. This product is mixed with water and a small amount of dishwashing liquid. The mixture is then sprayed on and dries to a white film on leaves, which is supposed to repel grasshoppers.

Food-grade diatomaceous earth (see warning, page 12) will kill grass-hoppers if they eat it. One recipe combines a cup of diatomaceous earth with a gallon of water plus two tablespoons of molasses. Spray this mixture onto plants. You will prevent most, but not all, damage with this method. Be sure to wash the harvest from all treated plants before eating.

Many birds love to eat grasshoppers, so keeping a birdbath close to the garden will attract many bird species. Be sure to keep it clean with regular scrubbing and refilling with fresh water. Chickens love a good insect dinner, too. If your zoning laws permit it, try keeping a few and letting them roam your garden. They will keep many other pests at bay as well (and supply you with fresh eggs).

Like aphids, grasshoppers are attracted to the color yellow. Place yellow sticky panel traps away from your garden to catch any grasshoppers in the vicinity. Panel traps are available commercially. You can also make your own sticky trap using a yellow paper or plastic plate spread with Tanglefoot. Just remember it will need to be *very* sticky to hold a grasshopper, and it's essential to keep pets away from these very sticky traps. Tanglefoot, which can be purchased at most local garden shops, can be hard to remove. Wear gloves when applying and disposing of the traps. Another yellow trap method is to take a bucket partially filled with soapy water and float pieces of yellow plastic on the surface. The grasshopper goes for the yellow attractant and drowns in the water.

You can also make a bait trap for grasshoppers. Combine nine parts water and one part molasses. Some gardeners suggest also floating a small amount of canola oil to make a film over the water as an extra attractant. Place this solution in a small bucket and place the bucket near your garden.

There are several beneficial insects that will prey on grasshoppers, such as paper wasps, tachinid flies, robber flies, and parasitic wasps. Try planting cilantro, dill, caraway, and anise to attract some of these beneficial insects to your garden.

Always practice good garden cleanup each year. Remove weeds and old plants in and around your garden that provide a habitat for the grasshoppers and other pests. Then, before planting, cultivate the soil well to expose grasshopper and other pest eggs to predators.

Short- and long-horned grasshoppers

Grasshoppers and crickets belong to the family Orthoptera and grasshoppers to the suborder Caelifera. There are many families within this order. The family Acrididae is the predominant family of grasshoppers. Ten thousand of the eleven thousand species of the entire suborder Caelifera belong to this one family. The Acrididae are best known because all locust or swarming grasshopper species belong to this family.

Grasshoppers are often divided into short- and long-horned grasshoppers. The horns are really the grasshopper's antennae. Long-horned grasshoppers have antennae longer than their bodies; these species are usually large, often nocturnal, and mostly plant eaters. The short-horned varieties have antennae shorter than their bodies and are active during the day. Most agricultural pest grasshoppers are in this group.

All life stages of the grasshopper look the same—except the egg, of course. They have long narrow bodies, with big hind legs for jumping, chewing mouthparts, and large eyes. Only the adults have wings, and most grasshoppers overwinter as eggs in the soil. Grasshoppers have one to two generations per year.

Grasshopper populations tend to rise and fall. Locusts are known to breed quickly when conditions are favorable and can lay waste to entire fields quickly. There are many known historical locust swarms, and locusts formed one of the plagues of Egypt.

As destructive as grasshoppers are, there are a few species that are predators. They have modified front legs to grasp their prey.

Grasshoppers often become prey themselves. Several cultures consume grasshoppers, which are high in protein. In a Beijing market, you can find grasshopper on a stick proudly displayed. In Mexico, *chapulines* (grasshoppers) are eaten not only for their protein but also for their vitamins and minerals. If you visit the Middle East, you may be offered a snack of grasshoppers that are boiled in hot water with salt and left in the sun to dry.

GREEN FIG BEETLES

Giant green iridescent beetles are whizzing past your head, and you discover they are heading for your prized grapevine or fruit tree.

Beating the beetles

Keeping your garden area clean of old plant clippings and prunings will help keep this beetle's population down by eliminating places where the beetle can lay its eggs. No beetle eggs in your yard means no adult beetles later.

Beetle larvae like the tender roots of lawns, and in heavy lawn infestations, soaking the lawn with soapy water will bring many of these grubs (or immature beetles) to the surface so you can pick them up and discard them. Many species of jays love to eat the grubs and will wait patiently for you to expose them.

In areas under trees and vines where you know there are beetle grubs, you can use clear plastic sheeting to catch many emerging adults. Place the plastic sheeting under the trees in late spring, and seal the edges with two-by-fours weighed down with rocks or bricks. Tape sheeting around tree trunks and seal well to the bark. When the beetle adults begin to hatch from their pupal cells, you will be able to see them at the soil surface through the clear plastic. Now you'll be able to capture many adults before they mate and produce more grubs. The adults aren't very fast and you can pick them up easily when one edge of the sheeting is rolled back. Dispose of the adults by dropping them into a bucket of soapy water.

Bait buckets can be placed near trees or gardens to lure the adult beetles. Fill a large bucket half-full of water, add a tablespoon of malt extract and a cup of molasses or some old fruit such as overripe bananas, and allow it to ferment. The beetles will go after the bait, fall into the bucket, and drown.

Many people who have compost piles actually find the beetle grubs to be very beneficial. The grubs aerate the pile and move a lot of decaying material through their bodies, turning it into usable compost. However, care must be taken to remove these grubs in early summer before they reach adulthood.

A beetle of many names

Green fig beetles, also called green June beetles or fruit beetles (*Cotinis nitida*), are common in warm climates of the United States. The adults are about one inch long and very thick-bodied. The adults are known to eat the leaves and fruit of many garden plants; their favorites are peaches, nectarines, apricots, pears, apples, figs, grapes, melons, and tomatoes. The large white larvae can be pests, causing damage to the roots of lawn grasses and many ornamental and vegetable plants.

Green fig beetles pass the winter in the larval stage, feeding on roots deep in the soil. By midspring, the grubs reach full size and dig a cell in the soil. This is where the larvae will spend their pupal stage. In July and August, the new adults will emerge to feed on fruit and foliage.

The eggs of the beetle are laid in dead vegetable matter, which the new larvae will feed on until winter, when they go underground. Keeping your garden clean will deprive this beetle species of a place to grow.

GYPSY MOTHS

The trees in your yard will display the telltale signs of a gypsy moth invasion: what was once a beautiful tree has been reduced to bare limbs in a few days' time. It may be too late for that tree, but there is help for the trees that still have leaves left on them.

Going on the attack

The gypsy moth was accidentally released in the United States in 1869 by a naturalist who was interested in using it to develop a disease-resistant silkworm, and it has since defoliated millions of acres of trees in the eastern part of the United States. If you live in an area that has gypsy moths, you should plan your attack on this pest early in the spring. Controlling the population is an essential tactic in keeping the damage to a minimum. Gardeners in the West, where the gypsy moth is not established, should also be on the lookout for this very destructive insect and report any suspected gypsy moths to their local agricultural officials.

The first step in controlling this moth is to remove all egg masses from trees, outdoor furniture, and buildings. Each egg mass ($1^1/2$ inches long and $3/4$ inch wide) contains up to a thousand eggs and is covered with buff-colored hairs from the abdomen of the female. The eggs are laid in the summer months between July and September and should be destroyed on sight.

The larvae, which are quite distinctive (see "The life of a gypsy," page 57), hatch in the spring and begin eating and doing damage to many species of trees immediately. If the egg mass was not laid on a tree trunk, the caterpillar will search for the nearest tree victim. The caterpillars' favored tree species are alder, apple, aspen, basswood, birch, hawthorn, oak, and willow. If their favorite trees are not available, the caterpillar will also attack beech, black gum, cherry, hemlock, hickory, hornbeam, larch, maple, pine, sassafras, and spruce. A burlap band placed around tree trunks can catch many caterpillars trying to go up into the tree to feed.

To use burlap banding, take a wide (two feet or so) piece of burlap, long enough to go around the tree with a bit of extra for overlap, and tape it around the tree trunk about two feet up. Tie a string or cord around the middle of the burlap. Remove the tape from the burlap and fold the upper portion down over the cord and lower portion. This is now a caterpillar trap! When the caterpillars try to climb up into the tree, they will get caught in the fold of the burlap. Check and remove caterpillars daily. You can also place a sticky substance (such as Tanglefoot) around the tree trunks. These bands are messier to use, but they work in much the same way as the burlap band and do not require daily checking.

Unfortunately, there are only a few natural enemies of the gypsy moth here in the United States. Its best-known enemies are the wasps *Hyposoter fugitivus* and *Apanteles schizurae*. The females of these wasps attack the caterpillars and lay their eggs in them. The eggs of the wasps then hatch and feed on the caterpillar from the inside, eventually killing it. You can encourage these wasps by planting flowering plants that produce lots of nectar.

Other predators of the gypsy moth are the *Trichogramma* wasp, which attacks the eggs of the moth, and spined soldier bugs, which will also attack the moth itself. Scientists are still studying many natural European enemies of the gypsy moth for application here in the United States.

In recent years, controlling the gypsy moth has been made easier with the use of the bacterium *Bacillus thuringiensis* (Bt). Spray Bt as soon as you see any caterpillars. It is very effective, but it takes a few days to do its work. Pheromone traps for adults, which reduce the numbers of breeding moths, are also commercially available. The traps use a sex attractant to lure the moth into the trap, where a sticky substance immobilizes it.

A fungus, *Entomophaga maimaiga*, which was first introduced into Virginia, has shown it is not the answer to eradicating the gypsy moth outbreaks in North America. However, studies have shown that it is a very important natural enemy, and with continued use it will have the long-term effect of decreasing high gypsy moth populations and in turn, it is hoped, will decrease the frequency of gypsy moth outbreaks.

The life of a gypsy

The gypsy moth (*Lymantria dispar*) is a member of the tussock moth family, and it earned its name by being a notorious hitchhiker. Unwitting humans transport the egg masses that the moths lay in trailer hitches, lawn furniture, and wheel wells. The gypsy moth and its relatives are serious pests of forest and shade trees.

The adult moths do not feed—their sole purpose is to mate and lay eggs. The eggs are laid by the female moth, which looks different from the male. The female is white with dark tan to brown inverted "V" markings on her wings. She has a wingspan of about two inches and is a poor flyer, if she flies at all. The male, which is smaller than the female, is dark brown with a black wavy pattern on its wings.

It is during its caterpillar stage that the gypsy moth causes all the damage. When the eggs hatch, the small caterpillars spin silken threads on which they can sail through the air by catching the wind. The caterpillars are easy to identify by the colored dots on their backs—first five rows of paired blue dots, then six rows of paired red dots. There are also tufts of hair along the sides.

When the caterpillars reach full size, about two inches in length, they form into pupae in the cracks and crevices of their host tree. The adults soon emerge to start the cycle all over again. Luckily for farmers and gardeners, the gypsy moth has only one generation per year.

HARLEQUIN BUGS

At first glance, you think you see large ladybird beetles (ladybugs) crawling on your prized cabbage. But wait, they aren't ladybird beetles—they're colorful stick bugs with black and orange markings. The beautiful harlequin bug isn't a beneficial addition to your garden at all—it's after your cabbage.

Harlequins don't clown around

The strikingly colored harlequin bug (also called the cabbage bug, calico bug, or fire bug) is definitely destructive to cabbage and other cruciferous crops in your garden. Yellowish patches on the plant's leaves, caused by the insect's feeding, are generally the first signs of damage you'll notice. In heavy infestations, the entire plant can be sucked dry and die.

Before planting your first seedlings in the spring, you should be thinking of how to keep this pest in check before its population can build up. Harlequin bugs like plenty of ground cover in which to breed and lay their eggs. A clean and neat garden will go a long way in keeping the population down. However, no matter how clean your garden is, if you live next to an open weedy field or have a neighbor whose yard is a jungle, you may have harlequin bugs. Harlequin bugs love mustard, and in California, where I live, this is a common weed. Concentrate your efforts on eliminating this weed early on, if you can, and don't plant mustard in your garden (except as a trap crop).

Trapping may be a good next step to try if harlequin bugs persist in your garden. A trap crop also works well with these insects. Because they like cabbage and mustard, plant some just for them. Unlike aphids, harlequin bugs are fast runners, and if you pull the plant up to rid yourself of these bugs, you may actually spread them around. It is wise to first spray the bugs on the plant with a strong insecticidal soap; then, while the bugs are stunned, remove the plant. Dunking the plant in soapy water right after pulling it will ensure that all the bugs are dead before you dispose of the plant.

The parasitic wasp (*Telenomus*) is an important natural predator of the harlequin bug. Its primary target is the eggs of the bug. There is also a species of parasitic fly in the Tachinidae family that attacks the harlequin's eggs and nymphs.

You can also reduce the population of harlequins by handpicking egg masses when you see them on leaves. The eggs are easy to identify—they are packed neatly together and resemble tiny white barrels ringed with black bands.

A harlequin's life

The harlequin bug (*Murgantia histrionica*) is a member of the true bug order, Hemiptera. Unlike other insects we call bugs, only the members of this order should really be called "bugs." True bugs have a first pair of wings that fold flat over the back of the insect. The word *Hemiptera* actually means "half wing." These wings, called *hemelytra*, are usually leathery toward the base and membranous at the end and resemble a shield held on the back. True bugs also have sucking mouth parts, called beaks, that they use to pierce plants. Some species—like the harlequin's cousin, the bedbug—also use the beak to pierce human skin.

Adult harlequin bugs overwinter in plant debris and emerge in the spring to lay their unique barrel-shaped eggs. The eggs are usually laid on leaf surfaces, in clusters of at least ten. The eggs hatch into nymphs that look like miniature adults and can disperse rapidly to feed on desired plants. Both the adults and the nymphs are pests to the gardener.

 ## JAPANESE BEETLES

You've just put in a new lawn, and you're ready for that first backyard barbecue, but suddenly you see brown patches appearing in your grass. Closer inspection shows small white grubs chewing on the roots. White grubs can signify many kinds of beetles, so how do you know whether your yard is infested with Japanese beetles? If it's May or later, look around your yard for the telltale damage of the adults. Leaves of shrubs and plants that have been chewed will look like lacy skeletons, and you may also see some small, metallic green and copper beetles, with six white tufts along their sides, feeding on your fruit.

Crashing their lawn party

The best defense against the Japanese beetle is a good offense, so targeting the larvae early will achieve good results. In the past, broad-spectrum
insecticides were poured on lawns in an effort to control this pest. A breakthrough in controlling Japanese beetles without harsh chemicals came
when milky spore disease was discovered. This disease is caused by a bacterium (*Bacillus popilliae*) which, when applied to lawns and around trees
and shrubs, effectively kills the immature larvae. Unlike insecticides, the
milky spore disease kills the grubs without hurting earthworms, beneficial
soil-dwelling organisms, or natural enemies of the beetle larvae that live in
the soil. It is recommended that yearly treatment be established to provide
long-term control for this pest.

Success has also been found with the release of parasitic nematodes. Two
that have been particularly effective are *Steinernema glaseri* and *Heterorhabditis bacteriophora*. These nematodes work best when applied to warm, moist
soils, and may not be as effective in early spring control. Most nurseries recommend applying nematodes in late spring or early summer.

Once the adult beetles emerge, your strategy needs to change. Commercial traps are available that use the female's pheromone or sex attractant to
lure the males. These traps are useful in determining if you have Japanese
beetles in your yard or how bad your infestation is. It is best to place traps
away from your prized plants, because the trap will attract the beetles.

If you determine that you do indeed have the dreaded beetles, a simple
and effective control measure is to dislodge and drown them. Early in the
morning, when the beetles aren't very active, knock them from shrubs and
branches onto a sheet and dump them in a bucket of soapy water. This process is time-consuming, but if done daily during peak infestations, it can
provide a good measure of control.

Harvest your garden frequently. The hungry beetles are attracted to
overripe and rotting fruit. Sometimes this means harvesting when vegetables like tomatoes are underripe and allowing them to ripen indoors. If you
love tree- and vine-ripened fruits and vegetables, try covering with crop
covers or placing paper bags over fruit and tying off with a piece of string to
prevent the beetles from feeding on them.

A great natural enemy of the Japanese beetle is the *Hyperecteina aldrichi* tachinid fly. If you have the pest beetle, then you probably already have the fly, so you don't need to do anything special to attract it. The adult tachinid fly feeds on flower nectar and pollen, and honeydew secreted by certain insects. Tachinids are sensitive to pesticide spraying (like many beneficial insects that feed on flower pollen and nectar), so avoiding pesticide use can prevent a decline in this helpful fly's numbers.

The beauty is a beast

Japanese beetles (*Popillia japonica*) have long been a pest in the northeastern part of the United States. These striking scarab beetles are about $^1/_2$ inch long, with stout bodies of metallic green. Their wing covers (*elytra*) are coppery in color, and they have white tufts of hair sticking out along their sides. So far, efforts to keep this pest from establishing itself in the West have been successful, and agriculture officials are ever on the alert for it.

The Japanese beetle larva causes most of its damage by feeding on the roots of grasses and tender plants. Because the larvae live underground, treatment is difficult. You can find the grub usually living about two inches below the soil surface. The grub stage occupies most of the life cycle of the beetle, with the adult beetle emerging from the ground around May or June.

Adult Japanese beetles like to congregate on plants and trees to feed and to find a mate. They can cause damage to many types of trees, vines, and bushes, including apple, black walnut, American chestnut, elm, grape, and rose, and they also feed on mature tree fruit, leaving it unsightly. After mating, the adult female lays her eggs in the soil, leaving the eggs to spend the winter underground and hatch in the spring to begin the cycle again.

 ## MEALYBUGS AND SCALE INSECTS

Little barnacle-like bumps about $^1/_6$ to $^1/_4$ inch long are appearing on your citrus trees. Your neighbor has also found bumps on his apples, figs, grapes, pears, and some ornamental shrubs. Though it may appear to be a plant disease of some kind, most likely you are looking at an insect pest, probably mealybugs or scale insects, which suck the juices right out of the plant.

Getting rid of the little suckers

Dislodging the insects from their host plants is quite an effective control. A strong spray with the hose will remove a great number of the pests. For small infestations, try touching a cotton swab dipped in alcohol to the insect, which should die in a few days. On larger infestations, wiping the insects with a rag saturated in alcohol will also work—just be careful not to burn your plants with the alcohol. You can also use oils to suffocate the insects, especially scales—in the winter, try dormant oils; in the summer, use special oils that won't burn the leaves. Check at your local nursery for the best oil to use.

Many parasitic wasps, lacewings, hover flies, and ladybird beetles are natural enemies of the mealybug and scale. The vedalia ladybird beetle (*Rodolia cardinalis*) preys on cottony-cushion scale, a serious pest of citrus trees. A beetle appropriately named the mealybug destroyer (*Cryptolaemus montrouzieri*) has been introduced in many areas to control these insects. Check with your local nursery to see whether the purchase of these predators would be beneficial in your area.

Controlling ants is very important in controlling mealybugs. Just as with aphids, ants will defend mealybugs from predators and use the honeydew they produce for food. See page 32 for information on controlling ants.

Stuck for life

Mealybugs and scales are closely related; they are both members of the insect family Coccidae. The armored appearance of these insects is caused by the waxy material they exude as a covering for their entire body. They do damage to plants by inserting their mouth parts and sucking out the plant's juices.

Their ability to harm great numbers of plants is a result of the large numbers of young they can produce. It has been estimated that one female of this family can produce up to thirty million young in one year!

In general, both mealybugs and scales have very similar life cycles. Females produce a waxy egg sac and, in some species, give birth to live young. In some species, the egg sac is deposited on a stem; in some others, the female carries the eggs under her shell until they hatch. Newly hatched nymphs have legs, but once they begin feeding on a plant, they start to secrete their covering. Scale insects become fixed to the plant at that spot, but some mealybugs can still move about, although they're quite sluggish. The females remain in this fixed state their entire lives. The male, when nearly grown, becomes an active, two-winged insect that looks like a tiny fly. At that stage, the male is incapable of feeding; his sole job is to mate with a female.

MOSQUITOES

You can hear them coming; they're like bombers on a desperate mission. Their sneak attacks are sometimes so good they've come and gone before you notice they've attacked you. But the bites they leave behind will remind you for days that they've achieved their mission: extracting your blood in order to complete their reproductive cycle.

Grounding the bombers

There are many strategies for repelling mosquitoes and preventing them from lighting on you and biting. Many commercially available products can be quite effective at repelling mosquitoes when used properly. Studies have shown mosquitoes are actually attracted to the carbon dioxide you breathe out; they can "smell" it in the air. Many of the mosquito-repelling scented products mask our carbon dioxide smell and work quite well. Citronella candles are a popular choice for repelling mosquitoes around the yard. They are known to provide good protection from mosquitoes, but only for a limited distance around the candle. Lemongrass contains citronella and can be planted in many landscape designs. Other plants claimed to be repellent are citrosa geraniums, horsemint, marigolds, and catnip. For indoor mosquito protection, try growing some of these plants indoors—or even bringing in a bouquet from outside. In addition to repelling mosquitoes, eucalyptus, mint, and rosemary also repel fleas, ticks, and gnats.

Start an herb garden and let it do double duty—herbs that are good in cooking can, when planted in hanging baskets near doors and windows, help keep pesky mosquitoes out of your house. Some good choices are basil, lavender, sage, rosemary, and thyme. These herbs can be rubbed directly on the skin and provide protection. When you barbeque or light your fire pit tonight, try breaking off a piece of rosemary and placing it on the hot coals. The scented smoke will repel the creatures. Try this idea with other herbs, too.

> Who is most likely to be bitten by a mosquito? Studies have shown the most likely target is a male who is overweight and has type O blood.

There are mosquito traps on the market to keep the buzzing insects away from you. One trap uses a pheromone to lure the mosquito into it. The mosquito can't get out and falls to the bottom and drowns.

Mosquitoes need water in which to lay their eggs, so be sure to eliminate all outdoor standing water. Check around your yard for places that water can collect. Look for potted plants in saucers where water stands, old birdbaths—even children's toys can be a mosquito breeding ground.

Mosquito fish (*Gambusia affinis*), which eat mosquito larvae, can be added to ponds to keep mosquitoes in check. In some areas, you can obtain the fish directly from your county agriculture department. Mosquito dunks are disks that are placed in ponds and other water sources to control mosquito larvae. The dunks contain a strain of *Bacillus thuringiensis israelensis* (Bti), a soil-dwelling bacterium that is effective at killing mosquito larvae, fungus gnats, and blackflies, while not harming other organisms. Bti also comes in liquid and granulated forms. An old-fashioned method of control that works well on very small bodies of water is to float a thin layer of mineral oil on the surface. This works by cutting off the oxygen to the breathing tubes of the larvae, killing them. Do *not* use oil film in ponds if you have fish.

There are many home remedies people claim work very well. These work by confusing the mosquitoes' chemical sensors. The problem with most of these is that they usually don't repel very long. Here are a few of the many out there: Scented clothes dryer sheets are said to be a great repellent; when you're out recreational fishing, try pinning a sheet to your shirt or hat or wiping the sheet across your skin. Rubbing the skin with Vicks VapoRub, pure vanilla extract, or Avon's Skin So Soft bath oil are also popular remedies. Soaking in a bath for fifteen minutes with two capfuls of chlorine bleach added is said to work wonders. Be careful not to get the chlorine solution in your eyes. When eating outdoors, place a bowl containing lemon dishwashing liquid or a pot of lemon balm on a table to keep mosquitoes away.

They want to suck your blood

Only the female mosquito bites. She needs blood to complete her reproductive cycle and lay her eggs. Unfortunately, her bite is not just uncomfortable; it can be dangerous. Mosquitoes are a serious public health concern worldwide; it is estimated that mosquitoes transmit diseases to over sixty-nine million people per year. Probably the best-known disease mosquitoes carry in their saliva is malaria, which is found in tropical areas. A relatively new disease in the United States that is also carried by mosquitoes is the West Nile virus, first introduced in 1999. It affects not only humans but several kinds of animals, including birds and horses.

A very interesting study showed that mosquitoes are attracted to the color red. So if you are sensitive to mosquito bites, wearing the color red may not be a good color choice when mosquitoes are active. Also avoid wearing a dark color, which heightens contrast between you and your surroundings and can make you a mosquito target.

Stopping the itch

Once you've been bitten, try these remedies:

- Apply calamine lotion or any other anti-itch cream. One homeopathic ointment is called Ssssting Stop.
- Dab a bit of ammonia on the bite.
- Place a liquid bandage over the bite.
- Place an ice pack on the bite.
- Moisten the bitten area with water and apply salt. This stings a bit, but when the salt is dry the itch is supposed to be gone.

- Make a paste of equal parts baking soda and water and apply it to the bite.
- Mix 1 tablespoon of Epsom salts in hot water. Chill the solution and dab it on the bite.
- For severe itching, your doctor may recommend an oral antihistamine.

 ## ROSE SLUGS (SAWFLIES)

Oh no! Your roses looked great the last time you looked at them, but now the leaves have lots of small holes between the leaf veins—in fact, the leaves are looking like skeletons. Sounds like your problem is the rose slug, which is actually not a slug but the larva of a primitive wasp called the sawfly.

Larval damage

When the rose slug hatches, it begins feeding on the green parts of leaves, leaving holes that look like little windows, because at first it does not eat the clear membrane of the leaf. As the insect larva grows, it can eat the whole leaf like most caterpillars, leaving typical feeding damage.

Watch your roses carefully and pick off any leaves that show the first signs of the caterpillar. This may be all you need to do if you catch the problem early. If the problem is more severe, look carefully on the undersides of leaves for the caterpillar, which can range up to $3/4$ of an inch long. Depending on the species of rose slug, they can be any shade ranging from green to black. Handpick any you see and destroy them to reduce their numbers. Usually handpicking is not the method of choice because you can only get a few at a time. Try washing them off with a strong stream of water. If just spraying water isn't working, insecticidal soap works well to control rose slugs. Be sure to spray the undersides of the leaves; that is where the rose slugs hang out.

Unfortunately, the common organic insecticide *Bacillus thuringiensis* (Bt), which controls caterpillars of butterflies and moths, will not work on the rose slug.

Rose slugs have many predators that like to eat them—such as birds, cara-bid beetles, and parasitoid wasps—that help keep their numbers in check. So use the most nontoxic remedy you can to prevent killing off the good guys.

Sawfly—or should we say sawwasp?

The rose slug or sawfly is neither a slug nor a fly; actually, it is an insect related to bees and wasps. The sawfly got its name from the sawing action the female uses with her ovipositor to create a slit in which she deposits her eggs. The adult lays a single egg in the leaf margin of a host plant. Sawflies that deposit their eggs in conifers can saw through wood. The sawfly looks like a wasp with transparent wings; however, it does not have a stinger or the characteristic wasp waist.

There are several different species of sawflies in North America, which feed on a variety of different host plants. A few hosts are pears, conifers, cherries, and roses. The sawflies that feed on roses are the bristly rose slug (*Cladius difformis*), the European rose slug (*Endelomyia aethiops*), and the curled rose slug (*Allantus cinctus*). Some of the sawfly larvae look a lot like a slug and actually have a slimy coating, thus earning them the "slug" name.

The life cycle of the sawfly follows a complete metamorphosis (egg, larva [caterpillar], pupa, adult) and is completed near the host plant. The number of generations of the rose slug varies among species, from one to six a year. Once the caterpillar is full grown, it will drop to the ground and pupate under the soil. There it will stay until it emerges as an adult sawfly to mate and deposit eggs anew on the host plant.

ROSE MILDEW

You love your beautifully cool coastal weather, but the night and morning low clouds that are so great for your straw-berries are causing a horrible mildew problem on your roses. What can you do?

A mildew solution

There are several simple fixes for rose mildew. It's best to combat the mildew before it starts, by mixing up our low-pH baking soda-and-water rose mildew solution. You can also try spraying clear water on your plants early in the morning, to knock off the spores responsible for the mildew. After mildew (or rust) has appeared, try using our stronger rust and mildew solution, which contains horticultural oil and kelp extract.

Rose Mildew Solution

2 tablespoons baking soda
1 gallon water
1 teaspoon commercial sticker/spreader (available at garden
    shops), or substitute 1 teaspoon liquid Turtle Wax or car wax

Mix together and spray on your roses.

Rust and Mildew Solution

2 tablespoons baking soda
1 gallon water
6 tablespoons horticultural oil
2 tablespoons kelp extract

Mix together and spray on your roses when rust and mildew appear.

SNAILS AND SLUGS

The telltale slime trails are appearing in your yard, and you're finding round holes in some of your favorite plants and shrubs. There's no doubt about it—snails and slugs (or both) have found a home in your yard.

Dead snails leave no trails

Snails and slugs can be effectively controlled in your garden or yard by several different methods:

- Ring plants that snails and slugs love, such as strawberries, with a thick layer of bran. (Yes, bran!) It can be bought at any feed store (or grocery store, though it will cost more there), and it works great to control snails and slugs. Besides being inexpensive, it is completely harmless to children, pets, and other animals. Food-grade diatomaceous earth (see warning, page 12) can also be spread around plants to control snails. When a snail or slug crosses the diatomaceous earth, the silica in the earth cuts the body of the snail or slug and kills it. If you live in an area where sawdust is available, it works in much the same way diatomaceous earth does. Unfortunately, all of these must be reapplied after a rain or heavy watering.

- One tried-and-true remedy is the old-fashioned beer trap. Place a saucer of beer (with the lip at ground level) in your yard or garden in the evening, and collect the little beer-lovers in the morning. Dispose of them in a bucket of salty water or give them to the ducks at your local pond; ducks love snails and will find them a treat! A yard with a duck will not have snails or slugs.

- Look for commercial snail baits with the ingredient iron phosphate. This chemical will kill the snails but is OK to use around pets. As with any bait, read and follow the directions carefully.

- Small children love to collect snails. You'll be surprised how fast the snails will disappear from your garden if you offer a nickel per snail!

- Traps made out of small cans are good at reducing the snail population. Bury the can almost to its rim and place a piece of decaying fruit at the bottom. Check and empty the can daily. (You may catch more than snails with this method.)

- Many gardeners, if they have a light infestation of snails, like handpicking for control. Handpicking works best at dusk, just after a rain, using a strong flashlight.

- Slugs and snails love to hide under things in the daytime. Use this knowledge to trap unwanted slugs. Place a few old flower pots, upside down and with the drain holes covered, in the areas where you know slugs live. Leave a crevice between the ground and the pot so the slugs can get under the pot. Check daily for hiding slugs and dispose of them.

- A small border of copper stripping can effectively keep slugs and snails out of your garden, as they will not cross copper. Tack the stripping along the edge of a raised bed frame or around tree trunks. Several commercial copper products are available at your local nursery for this purpose. If you live in an area where the giant banana slugs live, then slug control takes on a new meaning for you. Some of these giants can be six inches or more in length. The copper method works well for keeping banana slugs out, too.

- Much has been written lately on the benefits of purchasing decollate snails (*Rumina decollata*) to control the brown garden snail. Yes, these predaceous snails do eat many brown garden snails, and in the citrus orchards of Southern California they have provided excellent control of the brown garden snails without pesticides. But what do they eat when all the garden snails are gone? In gardens, the decollate snail will also feed on small plants, seedlings, and flowers when their favorite prey is not available. Also, decollate snails are not allowed in some areas of the United States. Check with your local agriculture department to see whether they are allowed in your area before purchasing them, and keep in mind that they may attack your plants after they've taken care of your brown snail problem.

Moving slowly through life

Snails and slugs are both members of the class of invertebrates known as mollusks. The mollusk class has over eighty thousand species worldwide that live both on land and in water. Most people find snails and slugs pretty disgusting, but they have a few cousins, including clams, oysters, and abalones, that are much-desired food sources for humans.

Slugs are basically snails without shells. Both move on one muscular foot, gliding on mucus slime. This mucus dries and leaves the silvery trails with which we're all familiar.

Snails and slugs feed on decaying matter and fresh plants. They do most of their damage to young seedlings and low-growing fruits, such as strawberries. In an orchard, snails and slugs would be of some benefit if they ate only the fallen rotting fruit, but they will climb a tree for fresh fruit as well.

SOW BUGS

Most people have seen small sow bugs (also called pill bugs), which like to hide in dark, damp places, and haven't thought much about them. However, if you decide to plant strawberries in your garden, you may soon be quite aware of the damage these critters can cause.

Sending sows south

Sow bugs need a moist environment of damp, decaying plant material in order to live. Keeping your garden clean of dead leaves and being water wise will go a long way toward reducing the population of sow bugs. Not letting fruits and vegetables touch the ground will also help prevent damage from these ground dwellers. Placing vegetables on top of strawberry baskets is a good way to keep them off the ground while allowing air to circulate around them.

Strawberries are a favorite target for sow bugs. These low-growing plants provide everything a sow bug could want. The leaves of most strawberries lie directly on the ground, keeping the soil moist underneath. Of course the fruit is a great prize, especially if it is overripe. Any method you can use to raise the plants up a bit will help, but this isn't always possible with strawberries. Prune any old leaves immediately and use small rocks to keep the fruit off the ground.

> Ever seen a bright blue sow bug? These unusual critters aren't a different species—they just happen to carry a harmless nematode that makes them turn blue. Scientists still don't know why. Yet another mystery of the animal kingdom . . .

Spread food-grade diatomaceous earth (see warning, page 12) around the plants, $^1/_4$ inch deep and 2 inches wide. The sow bugs that try to cross the diatomaceous earth will pick up particles of earth, which will cut into their exoskeletons and eventually kill them. (This method works best on slugs and snails, which do not have exoskeletons. Keep in mind that by controlling slugs and snails, you can determine what damage, if any, the sow bugs are causing.)

Make a sow bug trap with an old flower pot. Turn the pot upside down in an area where you know there are sow bugs. Now lift up one side about $^1/_2$ inch by resting it on a small rock. The sow bugs will be attracted to the dark place, and you can dispose of the ones you catch in a bucket of soapy water in the morning. Black plastic placed on the soil around your plants will also deter sow bugs by making the soil too hot for them.

Land lobsters

Yes, that's right—sow bugs are related to lobsters and crayfish. They are land-dwelling crustaceans, not insects. Sow bugs have a segmented body covering that resembles shells. Most sow bugs are about $^1/_2$ inch long and have seven pairs of legs. They also breathe through gills, which is why they must have a moist habitat. Overall, sow bugs are beneficial to the environment. They play an important role in recycling organic matter, are often found feeding on decaying fruit, and will generally choose decaying plant matter over fresh.

SPIDER MITES

You see small dots moving on some of your plants. Closer inspection reveals minute "spider" webs and tiny light specks on some leaves. You're sure these weren't there a few days ago—it looks like a mite attack.

More mites make right

For particularly bad infestations of spider mites, you may want to release commercially available predatory mites. This can be a very useful method for control because these mites feed only on other mites—they don't eat plants. If their food—spider mites—does become scarce, they will simply starve or move along.

Many people wonder why they experience a spider mite outbreak just after spraying pesticides on their trees. Research on mites has shown that when they're exposed to certain pesticides (carbaryl and parathion), they will reproduce much faster than they normally would.

If you live in a dry area, it's important to sprinkle water on pathways around trees and gardens to keep the dust down. Spider mites, like other species of mites, love dry, dusty conditions, so adequate watering is essential to keep them away.

A simple spray of water from a hose can dislodge the mites from their host plants and reduce their population. Be sure to really blast the undersides of the leaves, too. If plain water isn't reducing the mite population enough, some of the new insecticide soaps on the market are good at controlling mites. Read the label and follow all instructions carefully, because some soaps can burn plants. If overhead watering (as opposed to ground or drip watering) is feasible in your garden, it will help keep mite populations down. This method is used successfully to control mites on grapes in the West.

When spider mites are a problem on houseplants, one effective method is to rub a cotton swab dipped in equal parts water and alcohol on the plant. If the infestation is mild, this is usually all that is necessary to control the beasts. Rinse the plant well after treatment to prevent burning.

The life of a mite

Mites are very small (about $1/50$ inch) and sometimes completely invisible on first inspection. Most people notice the damage done by mites before they notice the mites themselves. Generally, when mite damage reaches a noticeable level, you are talking about an infestation of millions of mites.

Mites belong to the same arthropod order as ticks (Acari) and are not insects. Spider mites are related to other pest mites, such as red mites, harvest mites (also known as chiggers or red bugs), and water mites. All mites have eight legs; insects have six legs.

Spider mites are usually a pale yellow or green. Much like bees, spider mites are able to control what sex their offspring will be. An unfertilized egg will become a male and a fertilized egg will become a female.

Mite populations fluctuate as weather conditions change. When the weather is warm and dry, the mites will multiply rapidly, sometimes going through ten or more generations in one summer. Cool, damp conditions greatly reduce the numbers of mites.

SQUASH VINE BORERS

You go out to your garden and part of your squash plant is wilted. It was fine yesterday when you watered it, but today it's limp. The culprit could be squash vine borers.

Pest lurking inside

Squash vine borers are primarily found east of the Rockies. The adult form of this pest is a moth, which lays eggs on the stems near the base of a squash plant. They love summer squash but have also occasionally been found in cucumbers and melons. The larvae, which are white with brown head capsules, hatch out from late spring to early summer and burrow into the stems of the plant, which become the vines. The feeding of these larvae causes tunneling that damages the vascular system of the plant. The plant can no longer move fluids through that portion of the vine, and the vine wilts.

To check for squash vine borer, cut a slit into the stem and look for the caterpillar. Also look for holes at the base of your plant. Although just one caterpillar per vine is typical, you may find more than one. Along with the caterpillar, you will find its droppings, called *frass*, which looks like sawdust.

Is there hope?

If you have caught the damage early, you can try to reroot the vine and save it. To do this, remove the borer and bury the cut portion of the vine, keeping the soil moist. If you're in time, the vine will put down new roots. In areas where borers are a big problem, gardeners have found that mounding dirt along sections of the vines encourages more roots to develop, reducing the borer's damage. This may save your plant long enough to get a nice crop of squash.

The best plan is to watch for the moths and check for the eggs around the base of the stems. Scrape off any eggs you find. Use yellow panel traps to check for the presence of the moths. Like other pests I have mentioned, they are attracted to yellow. Make your own panel trap with a yellow plastic plate sprayed with a sticky substance—spray mount for attaching pictures to matting works well—and tack this to a stake or fence. You can also use a yellow bucket half filled with water. Add a few drops of dishwashing liquid to break the surface tension so they can't get out.

Another effective method is exclusion. Place floating row covers over your plants and keep them there as long the adults are present. Anchor the cover with soil to prevent the borers from getting in. If there are a lot of borers present and your plants are still flowering, consider hand pollinating the squash flowers. To do this, use a paintbrush to rub the pollen off of the stamens of male flowers and deposit it on the central pistils of the female flowers.

Remove any plants killed by the borer promptly and destroy them. If you have a warm summer, try planting a second crop of squash after the moths have stopped laying eggs.

A boring life

The squash vine borer (*Melittia curcurbitae*), is a clear-winged moth that loves all kinds of squash and pumpkins. The adult moth closely resembles a wasp; it is about $1/2$ inch long and has an orange abdomen with black dots. It has four wings; the front pair is metallic green and the second pair, which rests under the first pair, is clear, making the moth look like it has only two wings. In the southern regions of the United States, two generations a year of the squash vine borer are common; in the colder northern states, they normally have only one generation a year.

The one-generation-per-year moths emerge from cocoons in the ground in the spring or early summer. The adults look for squash plants on which to lay their flat, brown eggs. The eggs hatch in about a week and start burrowing into the stem of the squash plant. The caterpillar will stay there, feeding happily, for four to six weeks until fully grown and ready to form a cocoon. The caterpillar then leaves the plants and forms its cocoon, one to two inches under the soil. It remains there until the following spring.

 # TOMATO HORNWORMS

You can't wait for the first tomato of the season, so every day you check your prized tomato vines, waiting for that hard-earned fruit. On a visit to your garden one day, you're horrorstruck to discover that a whole section of leaves is missing. What could do that? A closer look reveals black pellets on some of the leaves and on the ground. Surprise—you have a tomato hornworm lurking.

Taking the worm by the horns

Tomato hornworms are equipped with excellent camouflage, making them very hard to see at first glance. Stay in the area of the droppings, and soon you'll see a motionless caterpillar hanging onto a stem. These large caterpillars can be controlled quite well by handpicking.

A larger infestation may require additional treatment. The commercially available bacterium *Bacillus thuringiensis* (Bt) is very effective against hornworms and other caterpillar species, such as cabbage loopers. When sprayed on plants, the bacterium invades the caterpillars and kills them. It works best on small caterpillars, so some of the large hornworms may not be killed quickly and will still need to be picked off by hand.

The hornworm spends the winter in a pupal form in the ground. After you pull up plants in the fall, turning over the soil helps to bring these large brown pupae to the surface, where you can either discard them or leave them to be eaten by birds.

Hornworms have some natural predators, such as the *Trichogramma* and Braconidae wasps. To check whether you have any of these natural predators working in your yard, examine the backs of hornworms for attached white cocoons that look like fuzzy rice. Soon the cocoons will break open to reveal a small wasp that will search for another hornworm to lay its eggs on. When these eggs hatch, the larval wasps will feed on the hornworm caterpillar.

The life of a sphinx

The dreaded hornworm is really the immature form of the beautiful sphinx moth (*Manduca quinquemaculata*). This usually nocturnal moth is quite large; one species has a wingspan of five inches or more. They have long, narrow forewings, with a heavy body that tapers at both ends. The sphinx moth has been compared with the hummingbird and is even called the "hummingbird moth" in some areas, because its hovering feeding method resembles the bird's. The sphinx moth has a long proboscis, or tube, extending from its mouth, which it uses to suck nectar out of flowers.

The sphinx moth lays its pale green eggs on tomato plants as well as potato and tobacco plants. Soon the eggs hatch into hornworms, its larval form. So far we don't know whether the horn-like structure from which the hornworm got its name serves any real purpose, except perhaps to scare off potential predators. Hornworms, which also have a camouflaging striped pattern, can grow to four inches in length, so it doesn't take many to completely wipe out a tomato plant!

WHITEFLIES

Clouds of tiny white insects are appearing around your garden plants. Your citrus trees have a blackened appearance from a sooty mold on the leaves, and your hibiscus has white sheets of thick webbing hanging down under its leaves. It sounds like whiteflies have taken over your yard.

Battling a tiny enemy

Many of the methods for controlling aphids, such as the yellow sticky traps described on page 37, will also work for whiteflies. For best results, stake the traps at plant level, out of direct sun. Replace when dirty.

Nasturtiums are a favorite of whiteflies, so planting some may keep the whiteflies happy and away from your other prized plants. Marigolds, planted in and around the garden, are known to be a good whitefly repellent.

Natural predators like lacewings and ladybird beetles feed heavily on whiteflies. *Encarsia formosa*, a commercially available parasite, feeds on the whitefly in its nonmobile nymph stages. Handpicking the most heavily infested leaves off the plant will give the beneficial predators a greater chance of controlling the pests.

Giant whiteflies are a big problem in California but the release of a predatory wasp discovered in Mexico has greatly reduced the problem. Check the eggs of the whiteflies. If they are black, then the wasps have parasitized the eggs and the eggs will produce more wasps.

If you are still having problems with this pest, do not reach for a pesticide spray, even an organic one. First, try water. A strong spray of water every five days will break the life cycle and greatly reduce the whitefly numbers. When stronger measures are needed, a soapy water spray or even a commercial insecticidal soap spray may be in order. Treating the undersides of leaves is very important. Always check for burning with any soap product, and rinse the plant if necessary.

A water-alcohol solution (see page 79) is known to be an effective control for whiteflies. This spray also works well on houseplants that can't stand the strong hose spray method. You can also dab the solution on house plants with a cotton ball.

A small vacuum cleaner will suck up many nymphs and adults on your plants. Vacuuming works best in the morning, when the whiteflies are moving slowly. First, vacuum up some boric acid (a couple of tablespoons will do; see warning, page 10) to kill the flies when they arrive in the vacuum bag, or place the vacuum bag containing the whiteflies in a plastic bag in the freezer to kill them.

A commercial oil emulsion spray is one method for controlling whiteflies in large citrus trees. These are oils made from petroleum that kill whiteflies on contact by suffocation. However, oils are not species-specific and will harm the beneficial insects with which they come into contact. As with all methods of control for whiteflies, treating the undersides of leaves is very important. There are several oils on the market for this purpose. Many gardeners like to use a paraffinic oil, but check with your local nursery for the one that fits your gardening needs. Experts recommend avoiding the use of oils in very hot weather—you could literally fry the leaves on your plant.

Whitefly Control Spray

1 cup water
3/4 cup rubbing or isopropyl alcohol

Mix in a spray bottle and spray on plants.

Check for burning before treating the entire plant. Rinsing the plants after the spray has been on for a few minutes will help reduce the chance of burning.

Little fly, big trouble

These tiny ($^1/_{12}$ inch) flies are closely related to aphids and scale insects. Whiteflies are found worldwide and have been quite a problem for citrus growers in Florida and California. Cultivated crops, such as lettuce, have also been hit hard by whiteflies in recent years. Whiteflies are so named because of the fine white powder that covers their wings and bodies.

Whiteflies start their lives as tiny eggs ($^1/_{100}$ inch long) attached by short stalks to the undersides of host plant leaves. The nymphs hatch in four to twelve days and are called *crawlers*. In this stage, the whiteflies are able to move about on the plant. The crawlers soon begin feeding on the plant by inserting their piercing mouth parts. After feeding and growing, the nymphs molt to a legless form, which is a flattened oval resembling a scale or mealybug. The whiteflies go through two more molts and then emerge as adults. Three to four generations are produced in a season. The whitefly's unusual life cycle makes it one of the most difficult pests to treat.

WIREWORMS (CLICK BEETLES)

Something is eating the roots of your vegetables. You notice that your corn, beets, potatoes, strawberries, beans, and several other crops are not germinating well either. Plants are dying; your garden generally isn't doing well. It's time to check the soil for a wireworm invasion.

Tough to control

Wireworms are the larval form of click beetles. The click beetle adult is pretty harmless to plants, but the slender, yellowish-brown, hard-bodied wireworms that look a lot like a meal worm can be lethal. If you suspect wireworms, make a lure by taking a potato and poking a bunch of holes into it. Stick a bamboo skewer or small stick into the potato and bury it a few inches deep, with the stick sticking out of the ground. The stick helps you find the potato and allows you to retrieve the potato without touching it. Pull up the potato in a couple of days and check to see whether wireworms are happily eating it. This lure makes a great trap too—just repeat this process, or place potatoes cut in half, cut side down, along rows to catch wireworms. Shake off any captured wireworms into a bucket of soapy water.

Wireworms can be a big problem to new gardens if the garden soil was recently covered by lawn or turf grass, because click beetles like to lay their eggs in grasses. If you plan to remove lawn or a grassy area to make a garden area, do not just turn over the lawn into the soil. It is best to remove the grass or lawn and completely compost it before returning it to the garden area soil. It is also a good idea to turn over the soil underneath the lawn and leave it open for a few weeks. This helps get rid of wireworms and grass seeds in the soil. Once you turn over the soil, the seeds will germinate, and removing them now will greatly reduce weeding in your garden.

Another good trap for wireworms is to place boards in between rows. The cooler ground under the boards attracts many different insects beside wireworms. Just lift and destroy all the pests you find.

A trap crop of corn, a favorite of wireworms, in areas with lots of wireworms can help. Plant corn to attract the worms away from other vegetables you want to grow.

Adult jumpers

Click beetles belong to the insect family Elateridae, and they got their name because the adults are capable of making a loud click sound and jump to avoid predators. You will be able to tell if you have an adult click beetle by placing it on its back; it will make a click sound and right itself. Click beetles have a spine that can be snapped into a corresponding notch that makes the sound. The adults are small, about $^1/_2$ inch long, brown or black, and usually nocturnal. They look a lot like beneficial predaceous ground beetles, which are found nationwide and are predators of cabbageworms, cutworms, slugs, snails, and many ground insects—but click beetles do make a clicking sound.

There are over nine hundred species of click beetle species nationwide and the adult form of the beetle is generally not considered a pest. However, several species of the larval form or wireworm are serious agricultural pests. These wireworms live underground and cause quite a bit of damage through their ability to find plants by detecting the small amounts of carbon dioxide released by plants into the soil. This allows them to quickly go from plant to plant. Another reason they are such pests is their ability to overcome and live through pesticide exposure, even after repeated exposures. Wireworms cause quite a bit of damage to agricultural wheat crops with their habit of going from plant to plant to feed.

Wireworms hatch from eggs laid in May and June and can reach a length of $1^1/_2$ inches. The wireworm has three sets of tiny legs, like most beetle larvae, which distinguishes it from crane fly larvae, which have a similar appearance. Wireworms are relatively long-lived insects, with some species living two to five years.

---

chapter four

Pet Help

 FLEAS

Welcome to flea season! It seems the little bloodsuckers have taken over both house and yard. Your pets are
scratching and biting themselves, and you and your children also suffer flea
bites while playing with the family dog.

Flea-fighting strategies

Fleas have always been a major problem for humans and animals; an article
by Texas A&M University estimated that Americans spend nine billion dollars on flea-fighting chemicals each year. In the past, DDT was routinely
prescribed to fight fleas, and people throughout the ages have gone to great
lengths to rid themselves of this dangerous pest. (One old recommendation
was to mop wood floors with kerosene.) The following are some less drastic,
more helpful ideas to keep those pesky fleas under control.

In areas of the house where pets are allowed, a sprinkling of borax on
the carpets and under the pet's bed will help keep flea numbers down by
desiccating (drying out) the fleas. Sprinkle the borax on by hand, or place
it in a flour sifter for a nice even application. Brushing the borax into the

carpet gets the drying agent deep into carpet fibers where the flea eggs and larvae like to live. Leave it down for several hours (or even several days, for heavy infestations) and then vacuum it up. It is best to keep children and pets off the carpet while the borax is down. For best results, use the borax treatment every time you vacuum during peak flea season.

Food-grade diatomaceous earth (see warning, page 12), like borax, can also kill fleas by drying them. It has an added benefit in that it can also puncture an insect's outer waxy exoskeleton and cause even more moisture loss.

When vacuuming, remember to change your vacuum bag often; if you have a heavy infestation, you should change it every time you vacuum. The vacuumed dust is perfect nourishment for the flea larvae you've just vacuumed into the bag. If you don't change the bag, you could be spreading fleas the next time you vacuum. To avoid changing the vacuum bag every time you vacuum, vacuum up a couple of tablespoons of boric acid (see warning, page 10) or borax, which will kill the flea larvae and adults that enter the bag.

D-limonene, a compound found in lemon peels, is a very effective repellent and insecticide for fleas (and for other types of insects as well). Veterinarians often recommend products containing this compound because, when properly diluted, treatment can be safe even for kittens and puppies. The easy homemade lemon solution on page 85 relies on the natural repellent action of d-limonene. Note: Just like people, animals (especially cats) can have allergies to lemons or any food item. If your pet starts shaking or vomiting after application of the lemon solution, promptly wash the solution off with a good shampoo. If the symptoms persist, get worse after washing, or are severe, consult your veterinarian immediately.

Eucalyptus can also be an effective flea repellent. Eucalyptus leaves or mulch placed under your pet's bed or house work just like cedar shavings to repel fleas. In areas with eucalyptus trees, substituting eucalyptus shavings for cedar shavings could be quite a savings. Eucalyptus can also be made into a "tea" (page 85) to be sprayed on your pet or around your pet's bedding or house to repel the fleas.

Remember: when using any product (like diatomaceous earth or borax) that contains dust particles, *always* wear a protective dust mask to avoid inhaling any potentially harmful particles, and *never* dust when children and pets are present.

Our Eucalyptus Flea and Tick Repellent recipe (see opposite) gives directions for making your own extract. You can also purchase eucalyptus oil or extract concentrate (at health food or pet stores) and mix it with water.

Flea combing can be an effective method of control, but the effort it takes to do it routinely sometimes makes the job seem impossible, especially if you have a long-haired pet. If you do decide to flea comb your pet, keep a jar of 70-percent alcohol or vinegar nearby and plunge your comb into it to kill the dislodged fleas. For effective combing, comb first with the grain of your pet's coat, then again against the grain.

Beneficial nematodes, which can usually be purchased at pet and home supply stores in the spring, can be sprayed in your yard, where they'll attack immature fleas. Read the Nematodes section in chapter 6 (page 126) for more information.

There are products on the market that you apply topically to your pet. They are basically chemical flea collars. One product's active ingredient is the common pesticide imidacloprid, which kills the fleas by affecting the flea's nervous system. There is no question that these topical flea controls are a great help to our pets that suffer with flea allergies and parasites. Consult with your veterinarian for the best product for your pest and contact the vet again if any redness or reactions occur after applying what's recommended.

Another chemical to control fleas is the ingredient methoprene, found in popular flea and tick prevention products. It is an insect growth regulator. This regulator prevents insects from becoming adults and producing eggs. Methoprene is used most widely to kill mosquitoes, which is an important measure in prevention of the West Nile virus.

In your yard, try planting fleabane to repel fleas. Fleabane is the common name for a number of flowering plants in the family Asteraceae, all bearing daisy-like flowers with golden disc flowers and violet rays.

Finally, if you have tried everything and nothing is working, maybe you don't have fleas. There are other insects that bite, like chiggers, mites, bedbugs, and spiders. To make a flea trap to check if fleas are your problem, hang a light directly over a shallow pan with a couple of inches of soapy water in it. The fleas (if there are any) will be attracted by the heat of the light, land in the water, and drown.

Lemon Flea Repellent

Peel of 2 large or 4 small lemons
1 quart water

Boil the lemon peels in the water for 10 minutes. Cool to a comfortable temperature. Sponge the lemon water on your pet and leave on for an hour or so. Rinse off. For heavy infestations, leave the lemon water on without rinsing. Repeat weekly, if necessary.

Eucalyptus Flea and Tick Repellent

About 20 fresh eucalyptus leaves
1 quart water

Boil the leaves in the water for 5 to 10 minutes. The liquid should have a strong eucalyptus odor. Cool, strain out the leaves, and spray on the liquid as necessary (pay special attention to your pet's feet). Some trees have stronger scents than others, so you may need to experiment with the number of leaves you use.

The hungry life of a flea

Have you ever gone on vacation or closed a resort house for the winter, only to find fleas waiting for you when you returned? Adult fleas that have had a host meal can live fifty to one hundred days without further food. Amazingly, adult fleas that have never eaten can live as long as two years without food.

Fleas are wingless, long-legged, jumping insects that live as parasites on animals. There are approximately 1,100 species of fleas worldwide, and they are easily identified by their bodies, which are flattened from side to side. Adult fleas rely on their great jumping power to escape their enemies. It has been calculated that a flea can jump two hundred times the length of its body, or about twelve inches. That would be like a cat jumping 14,400 feet! Most adult fleas are brown or black; the larvae and eggs are whitish.

Eggs of the flea are usually laid on the host and fall into the dust and crevices of the host's home or bed. The eggs usually hatch in two to fourteen days. One adult female flea may lay up to five thousand eggs in her lifetime. The larva of the flea, which resembles a maggot, is a scavenger that feeds on organic debris from your pet. After the larval stage, which can last from one to five weeks, a silken cocoon is formed, in which the larva transforms into the common adult flea.

Adult fleas emerge from their cocoons very hungry. Their only food is blood, and the little vampires immediately begin to look for a host meal. Adult fleas will feed once a day if the blood of a host is available. Whereas with mosquitoes only the females bite, both male and female fleas will bite a host for a blood meal.

FLIES

We're all familiar with the irritating antics of the common housefly. The sound of flies loudly buzzing against a window and the sight of them landing on your food can drive you crazy. Unfortunately, there are many types of flies, and each one of them has its own special way of tormenting you and your pets—especially horses. If you own horses, you've probably witnessed the constant aggravation flies can cause for the horse (and to you!). Some flies, such as stable flies and horn flies, will bite humans or beasts; others attack only fruits and vegetables. The house fly, which is simply looking for a free meal, serves mainly to annoy us.

Sending the annoying visitor packing

What would the fly swatter business be without flies? Who hasn't run for the swatter when the sound of a buzzing fly is just too much to bear any longer? Many owners of farm and stable animals have waged a never-ending war on these flying creatures. It is an unavoidable fact that horses, antelope, bison, and deer will attract flies no matter how clean their habitats are. Those of you with horses and cattle already know this firsthand.

Generally, the war on flies has been pretty frustrating, but good news may be here to help keep those flies at bay. It looks like a zookeeper in San Diego has built a better fly trap. (And you can imagine the fly problem a zoo might have, if it were left untreated!) The zookeeper tried many commercial fly traps, all with mixed results. Finally, a breakthrough came when the keeper noticed that the flies, especially the housefly and bottle fly species, were really attracted to old ground meat. A chunk of meat was placed into a commercial plastic bag fly trap, which contained a fly pheromone attractant, and a better fly trap was born.

> To catch a fly in your hand, or better yet to swat it with a fly swatter, try aiming at it from behind. Flies always take off backward—a little tip that will help you get your fly.

You can make your own version of this fly control method to use outdoors. Buy a hanging plastic bag fly trap with a pheromone attractant at your local nursery or home center. Many brands are available and any one of them will do. After preparing the trap according to the package directions, add a large quarter-sized piece of hamburger to the bag. Now hang the bag wherever you find flies. Sometimes it takes a few days for the hamburger to have just the right odor. Try placing different amounts of hamburger in your trap too, until it's perfect for your needs.

The short life of a housefly

The common housefly (*Musca domestica*) has one of the shortest life cycles of any insect and can produce many generations per year. A female housefly can lay up to five hundred eggs and each egg can reach adult maturity in only six to twenty days, depending on the temperature of its environment. The housefly is an ever-present pest to man, but an important source of food for many other insects and birds. Unfortunately, the housefly is known to be a carrier of many serious diseases, such as typhoid fever, cholera, anthrax, and dysentery.

Houseflies have only sucking mouth parts and hence cannot eat anything solid. In order for the housefly to eat something solid, it first must dissolve the solid food into a liquid form. To do this, the fly places its saliva (or sometimes its stomach contents) onto the solid food to partially digest it. Then the fly sucks up the dissolved liquid food. In this way, germs are passed and carried from one source to another.

 ## TICKS

Let's say it's a beautiful day and you and your favorite four-legged friend have just returned from a nice walk. While taking off his leash, you notice a tick. There is no mistaking the small flattened-oval shape of these irksome arthropods.

Protecting yourself from ticks

Ticks are one of the hardest creatures to defend against because, no matter how hard you try to repel them, you usually can't protect every area of your pet's (or your own) body. So carefully checking yourself and your pet after each outing is still a very wise idea.

During the summer months, when the weather is warm, we tend to wear less clothing. We don't like to go out wearing high boots with our pants legs tucked into them and long-sleeved shirts that are tight-fitting around the wrists and neck. But that's just the clothing necessary to guard against ticks. Loose-fitting clothing gives ticks good access to our bodies.

Ticks can burrow in any place on the body, but often you will find them where your clothing will help them get a good hold on you. Some of their favorite spots are at the tops of socks, inside shirts, and under the elastic of your underwear—so it is a good idea to check these areas in particular whenever you have been outdoors in tick habitat. Your furry pet, however, offers a head-to-toe selection of likely hideaways to the tick; pets are also especially vulnerable due to their penchant for uninhibitedly running through the bushes and rubbing up against tick-bearing vegetation.

If you do find a tick on yourself or your pet, the best method of removal is to grab the tick with a tissue close to the skin and pull it straight out. Do not twist the tick, or you risk breaking off its mouthparts in the skin. Apply an antibiotic ointment to the site.

With the growing awareness and fear of Lyme disease, tick repellents are becoming very popular. Many on the market now have been shown to work quite well. DEET is a popular repellent and fairly safe if used in small doses, but large doses can cause convulsions in pets and children, so it should be used with care.

A popular natural repellent is citronella (yes, the same compound that works against mosquitoes). Citronella is being used in some sunscreens, so these products will give you some mosquito and tick protection. Some products containing citronella also are claimed to protect against fleas.

Eucalyptus is an excellent repellent for ticks, fleas, and other insects, and you can make a simple and quite effective eucalyptus spray repellent (see page 85). Ticks are pretty resilient, so you may need to make the repellent a bit stronger by steeping the leaves longer. If making the repellent yourself is too much trouble, or if you live in an area without eucalyptus trees, you can purchase eucalyptus oil in your local health food store and dilute it to the strength you want. Keep in mind when using this solution that some dogs, and especially some cats, may not like the smell of eucalyptus. Start with a weak solution first and work up to a stronger-smelling solution if necessary.

Ticks are found throughout the United States, and in heavily infested areas, you should take precautions in your backyard to keep tick numbers down. Clearing away old dead underbrush and keeping your lawn watered and closely mowed is helpful. Trapping and disposing of mice on your property will take away one of the tick's favorite hosts and ideally send the ticks packing elsewhere.

Can ticks make you sick?

Ticks are arthropods with eight legs; they're not true insects. (But who sits and counts the number of legs a tick has when he finds one on his pet?)

There are two families of ticks in the United States: hard ticks (Ixodidae) and soft ticks (Argasidae). They are all parasitic and attack mammals, birds, and reptiles. Being bitten by a tick is not just annoying; the bites can also be quite dangerous. Ticks transmit diseases—including Rocky

Mountain spotted fever, Lyme disease, tularemia, and Texas cattle fever—
to humans and animals.

Ticks are small creatures, about $3/16$ inch long and usually dark brown
to bluish gray. An engorged female may reach a length of $1/2$ inch or more,
and one female tick can lay four to seven thousand round brown eggs on the
ground after she has fed on a host.

When the eggs hatch (about a month after they're laid), each tiny
$1/40$-inch larva climbs up to the ends of blades of grass and other plants to
wait for some passing animal to climb onto. Once on board, the larva will
feed on the animal (white-footed mice are a favorite of deer ticks at this
stage) for two to twelve days. The larva will then fall to the ground, shed its
skin, and become a nymph. The nymph now looks for a host. After feeding
for three to ten days on this host, again the nymph falls to the ground and
undergoes its final change into the adult form. Now the adult is looking for
you. It is only in the adult form that the tick attacks people. The entire life
cycle of a tick can take two to three years.

In case you're unlucky enough to be bitten by a tick, you should know
some of the symptoms of the serious illnesses they could carry in your area.
Contact your doctor if you have any of these symptoms:

Lyme disease: rash, chills, fever, fatigue, arthritis-like stiffening in the
joints, and severe headaches. Look for a bull's-eye red mark at the site of the
bite, but be aware that it does not always appear.

Rocky Mountain spotted fever: fever and a peculiar skin rash of grayish
or brownish spots usually appearing on the arms, legs, and body a few days
after the fever begins.

chapter five

Good Guys or Bad Guys?

BLISTER BEETLES

Most insects are not all good or all bad for human purposes—many are a combination of both. The blister beetle is a great example. Blister beetles, also known as oil beetles, show up when your vegetable crops start looking good. They are known to eat tomatoes, beans, beets, carrots, cabbages, corn, eggplants, melons, peas, peppers, radishes, spinach, squash, sweet potatoes, and turnips. Sounds like they could eat your entire garden, doesn't it? But they do have a good side—they eat grasshopper eggs.

Banishing the blister

There are many species of blister beetles, and many love to eat the leaves of various plants. They often show up in large numbers. Because this is a chewing insect, sprinkling the leaves of plants with food-grade diatomaceous earth (see warning, page 12) will help control the beetles. As with other insect pests, the diatomaceous earth works when it comes in contact with the insect's exoskeleton and absorbs the fats in the waxy outer layer, causing the insect to dry out. You can find food-grade diatomaceous earth online and at specialty stores. It has many uses, including a soil medium for bonsai plants. Swimming pool diatomaceous earth is not recommended, because natural diatomaceous earth is a light powdery substance, and when produced for swimming pool filters, it is heated and treated with soda ash to make it crystalline. The downside to this product is it works best if it stays dry; if it becomes moistened, it should be reapplied. Do not apply to flowers; this could adversely affect honeybees.

Many gardeners say handpicking is the best way to beat these beetles. If you do this, be sure to wear gloves, because blister beetles emit a toxin, cantharidin, which can blister skin. A better method is to use their habit of dropping off a plant and playing dead against them by placing a pan of water with a few drops of dishwashing liquid added under the plant and then quickly tapping on the plant. The adults fall into the water and drown.

Trap crops are a good idea, too. Plant calendulas, clover, pigweed, or any plant you have seen the beetles particularly like at the far corners of your garden or along a fence. Then, when the beetles are present, you can kill them by bagging the plants or by any other method you choose.

One method that would be good to try, if you have both the space and a big problem with blister beetles, is to plant rows wide apart from each other. Many farmers believe they do not like to cross wide areas.

Horseradish is known to repel blister beetles and will probably repel other insects as well. Mix prepared horseradish or ground horseradish root with water and spray on plants. Just remember to wash the plants thoroughly before eating or cooking.

A blistering life

Blister beetles are members of the Meloidae family, whose varied members can be found nationwide. The striped blister beetle (*Epicauta vittata*) is one of the most damaging; it can be found in all eastern states and portions of Canada. The adults like to feed together and eat the leaves and flowers of garden plants. As mentioned earlier, the blister beetle does have one redeeming feature: its larvae feed on grasshopper eggs.

Blister beetles have a complex life cycle called *hypermetamorphosis*. This means the larval stages have very different appearances. Females lay eggs in clusters of one hundred to two hundred in the soil where grasshoppers are found. The eggs hatch in about two weeks, and the larvae feed on the grasshopper eggs. It is estimated that blister beetles will consume up to 25 percent of grasshopper eggs each year. As the larvae molt, they change appearance. The legs and mouth parts start out long and become smaller and smaller with each molt. The larvae will molt five to seven times before they pupate in the soil. Adults emerge usually in great numbers in June and July, but some species can be present from April through October.

The adults are approximately one inch long and have a narrow body. They can be a solid color or striped. Colors range from metallic blue, green, copper, or rose to a striped black and yellow. Most blister beetles have one generation per year, and the adults live four to six weeks.

Blister beetles get their name from the toxin they produce, which can blister both human and animal skin. It is a good defensive mechanism against predators. The toxin, cantharidin, causes blisters in the mouths of livestock if eaten and damages the digestive tract. Several species of blister beetles love alfalfa, and if large numbers of blister beetles become entangled in the bales of alfalfa, this feed can be fatal to horses, which are particularly sensitive.

CENTIPEDES

You're out tending your garden one day, and as you move some debris, you see a slithery, multilegged, prehistoric-looking creature running for cover. It has too many legs to be an insect, so what can it be? A better question is, is it beneficial or not? It's a good chance that creature is a centipede—and a great predator of insects and small animals.

A good arthropod

The centipede is found worldwide in tropical and temperate climates. To date, approximately three thousand species of centipedes (class Chilopoda) have been named worldwide. Most North American species range in size from one to two inches long and feed on small insects, slugs, and worms. However, centipedes in the tropical zones can reach lengths of six to eight inches and feed on toads, snakes, and rodents.

Centipedes have a somewhat flattened shape, with one pair of legs for each body segment. Most are brown, but some are red, green, yellow, blue, or a combination of these colors. They are usually nocturnal and prefer to live in dark, damp places, like under rocks, bark, and debris.

An old wives' tale says that the bite of the centipede can be fatal to humans. Even though centipedes do release a toxin from their powerful jaws to help them catch their prey, much as a venomous snake does, no human death has ever been directly linked to a single bite from a centipede. The centipede's bite is said to feel like a very severe yellow jacket wasp sting.

It is unlikely that you can attract centipedes to your yard. But having some suitable habitat in your garden may help encourage any centipedes you already have to stay. An old board in a damp, shady spot might be all you need to keep a centipede on the prowl in your garden.

CRANE FLIES

Here they come—those giant flying "mosquitoes" that some people call mosquito hawks. Though they look like they could suck all the blood from a Chihuahua, they're actually harmless.

Harmless imitators

The family of crane flies (Tipulidae) is a diverse group of over 1,450 species, ranging in size from tiny to more than three inches in length. They are long and slender, with narrow wings and long, fragile legs. Some species closely resemble mosquitoes, but crane flies do not bite. Adults have a thin tube-like structure called a proboscis, which they use to feed on flower nectar, but very little is known about their feeding habits. Crane flies are not strong fliers and are often seen hovering in corners or bouncing against walls or windows.

Crane flies can be found in damp areas where there is plenty of vegetation. The larvae are mostly aquatic and feed on decaying plant matter. There is one species that does feed on living plants, but the damage it causes is usually minimal. There are also a few beneficial species that prey on other insects.

CRICKETS

The cricket in your house may be happily chirping for a mate, but you're not happy to hear this sound in the middle of the night. You climb out of bed and head for the noise, but as soon as you are close enough to figure out where it is coming from, it stops, only to start again when you return to bed. After a few nights of this, you're just about ready to call the funny farm.

A sticky solution

To capture midnight chirping crickets in your house, you'll need duct tape and a few pieces of dry dog (or cat) food. Pull off a piece of tape about two to three feet long and place it sticky side up on the floor, along the baseboard where you hear the chirping. Now place pieces of dog food on the tape about eight inches apart. Crickets love dog food, and when they walk on the tape to get the goodies, they should get stuck on the tape.

Many people believe crickets are good luck, so if you don't want to hurt the cricket, you can gently unstick him and deposit him outside where his chirping won't bother anyone.

Insect musicians

Male crickets and their cousins, the katydids, chirp to attract a mate and to defend their territories. They do this by rubbing a structure called a *file*, located on their leg, with a structure on their wing, called a *scraper*. On warm nights, the chirping of the males in search of a mate can go on for hours. Each cricket species sings a distinctive song, which a good listener can use to tell one cricket species from another.

The family to which crickets belong (Gryllidae) can be found throughout the United States. Crickets resemble small grasshoppers, but there is great diversity in the sizes and shapes they take. Ant-loving crickets are only three to five millimeters long and are found living in ant nests, whereas field crickets are close to an inch long.

Crickets can cause damage to many field crops and in some areas have been recorded infesting fields in great numbers. Tree crickets can also cause serious damage to small tree limbs and twigs by girdling the twig with their egg laying. Most crickets overwinter as eggs, which are generally laid in the ground or in vegetation.

DARKLING BEETLES (AKA STINK BEETLES)

What are those big black beetles that some people call stink beetles or, depending where you live in the United States, stinkbugs? Are they eating my garden? Considering their size, they must be doing a lot of damage.

Stinky scavengers

Darkling beetles may have delivered the ultimate insult when they first raised their behinds toward menacing humans and emitted a black fluid with a very disagreeable odor. Since then, they've been stuck with the awful name stinkbug.

Most of the 1,500 species of darkling beetles that live in North America are plant eaters, fungus eaters, or scavengers on decomposing wood or dead animal matter. For the most part, the big black beetles we see are scavengers of dead matter. They are very common under stones, garbage cans, and loose bark. The beetle usually doesn't do any harm to gardens, but instead is seeking shelter and dead material in the garden. However, a few of the smaller species have been known to become plant pests. Tidy gardens usually have very few darkling beetles.

In arid regions, the darkling beetle has taken over for the carabid or ground beetle, which preys on many pests. In this case, the darkling beetle can be very beneficial. The larvae of the darkling beetle are greatly prized commercially—they're the mealworms we buy for fish bait and supplemental bird food.

Darkling beetles have no wings, and their only defense mechanism is the smelly fluid they excrete. But certain species of darkling beetle raise their abdomens for a different reason. In the desert, where water is scarce, a darkling beetle will point its raised abdomen at an oncoming fog. The fog droplets condense on the beetle's abdomen, and when enough of them merge to form a water drop, it will run down the abdomen, straight into the beetle's mouth!

EUCALYPTUS LONG-HORNED BEETLES

You've noticed lately that the beautiful eucalyptus trees in your yard aren't looking so good. On closer inspection, you find that lots of sap is running down the trunks of the trees, and the branches and leaves are wilting and discolored. Is it a fungus? Perhaps, but it's more likely the damage can be attributed to the beautiful eucalyptus long-horned beetle.

Stopping the bothersome borer

It's the larval form of this large, lovely beetle (*Phoracantha semipunctata*) that causes all the damage to eucalyptus trees. Their boring activity under the bark and inside the tree makes treatment and eradication of the borer quite difficult. You usually do not know your trees have the borer until damage to the tree is visible.

Prevention and early intervention, when possible, are the best tactics. Check trees regularly for signs of borer attack. Start by looking under loose bark for borer eggs, entrance holes, and tunneling. The tunneling will look as if the wood has been burned with a branding iron; dark brown tunnels will radiate from a central area and suddenly disappear. Prune the limbs where these markings are found. Borers also love to attack stressed trees. A bit of extra water in the dry summer months and careful pruning of old and yellowing branches will help the tree remain strong and prevent an all-out borer infestation.

After pruning any areas of your eucalyptus trees where the borer has been found, be sure to seal all cuts to your tree and to dispose of the wood carefully. The borers can live in cut wood just as easily as live wood, so you may be raising the next generation of borer if you just leave the wood in a pile to dry. Many entomologists recommend that the wood be buried or burned to prevent the spread of the borer. However, if you like eucalyptus wood for your fireplace and don't want to completely dispose of it, remove as much bark as you can from the cut logs and branches and then stack the stripped wood on a clear plastic tarp. Completely cover and seal it in the plastic and leave it there for at least six months. This should kill most of the borers inside the tarp and keep out any that are looking for a home.

A long-horned life from Down Under

The eucalyptus long-horned beetle belongs to the beetle family Cerambycidae; there are 1,200 species in this country, all of which feed on plants or trees. This Australian beetle, introduced to California in the early 1980s, has been a growing problem. It has the potential for expansion to many areas outside of California where eucalyptus trees grow.

Most long-horned beetles have elongated cylindrical bodies and backsweeping antennae that are often two to three times longer than the body. They range in size from $^{1}/_{4}$ inch to over 3 inches in length; the adult eucalyptus long-horned beetle measures a little over an inch. Many adult longhorned beetles are brightly colored, and these usually feed on flowers. The eucalyptus long-horned beetle is dark brown with a cream-colored zigzag band across its back and feeds exclusively on eucalyptus wood.

The adult beetles lay their eggs in bark crevices, and when the eggs hatch, the larvae tunnel under the bark for a bit and then bore into the wood. The mature cream-colored larvae of the eucalyptus long-horned beetle grow to about $1^{1}/_{4}$ inches long and $^{1}/_{3}$ inch wide. By looking at the borer's tunnels, you can help identify which family of borer you have infesting your trees. This is important information in determining which treatment should be used for borers. Eucalyptus long-horned beetle larvae produce a round hole when boring.

Because the eucalyptus long-horned beetle was imported from Australia, it had no natural enemies when it arrived in the United States. However, work is being done to introduce predators of the beetle to this country and provide some much-needed natural control.

JERUSALEM CRICKETS

Sooner or later you'll see one, and it will take your breath away. The Jerusalem cricket is a large and ugly insect, but is it a friend or foe? It's so objectionable looking, it's easy to assume it must be able to devour an entire garden. But relax—it's a good guy to have around.

An ugly insect that really cleans up

The Jerusalem cricket belongs to the cricket subfamily Stenopelmatinae. This unusual cricket is found, for the most part, on the West Coast and is also known as a sand or stone cricket, potato bug, or *nina de la tierra* (child of the earth). It's wingless, nocturnal, and about two inches long, with a big head and stout legs. They don't look much like the common crickets we know at all, and they have no ability to produce sounds, like their noisy cousins the tree crickets. The Jerusalem cricket does, however, possess a pair of powerful jaws that can inflict a nasty bite if a person handles it.

These large crickets are basically scavengers that will clean up old plants and debris around your yard by eating the dead and decaying plant material. Damage to gardens is minimal, if any, because they prefer brown plants to green ones. The crickets prefer loose soil and rocks they can hide under during the day. Being nocturnal, they will remain unseen if the soil is left undisturbed.

The female Jerusalem cricket has mating habits similar to those of the female black widow spider. After the female cricket mates with the male, she'll kill him and then lay her eggs in a case that she'll carry around until the young hatch.

 ## SNAKES

It's hard to believe that those forked-tongued, legless creatures so many of us find a bit scary are beneficial. But it's true: even snakes that are venomous, like rattlesnakes, are predators that eat sizeable numbers of small animals. Snakes do the most good by helping to keep rodent populations down, thereby keeping rodents from invading our homes. Some snakes, like garter snakes, will even eat slugs and snails!

Uninvited guest

You generally won't know you have a snake visiting or living in your yard until you actually see it yourself. For many people, this is not a pleasant experience, but the truth is that these snakes are providing a service. Snakes keep rodent populations down. If you can't stand the thought of sharing your yard with a snake, then try one or all of the following ideas to make your yard less attractive to them.

If your yard is fenced, tack fine mesh wire along the bottom of the fence. For an extra measure of effectiveness, bury the wire about six inches deep before tacking it to your fence. The wire should extend up the fence eighteen to twenty-four inches. This will also keep out other intruders, like bunnies and skunks.

Keeping a well-groomed yard can also deter snakes from taking up residence. Snakes like to hide under piles of mulch, brush, rocks, or wood to escape the summer sun. If you don't provide any shelter, they will soon be on their way. Be sure to plug up any holes or cracks leading under your house, too!

Eliminating the rodent population in your yard will keep snakes from thinking your yard is a delicatessen. Check out pages 146–65 for tips on rodent control.

Venomous snakes

Most of us know that the United States has a few venomous snakes. The National Audubon Society's *Field Guide to North American Reptiles & Amphibians* lists 115 species of snakes in the United States, with only four kinds—rattlesnakes, coral snakes, water moccasins, and copperheads—classified as venomous. Good common sense (and an understanding of how they live, what they look like, and when they're active) will go a long way toward preventing a snake bite. But if you are bitten, some basic snakebite first aid knowledge will be very helpful. You may be surprised to learn that some of the standard techniques you've heard about have been proven to be useless—or downright dangerous.

- Remain calm.
- Try to immobilize the area, using a stick taped to an arm or leg, for instance.
- Wash the bitten area with soap and water, if available.
- Do *not* apply a tourniquet or ice to the bitten area.
- Do *not* cut the bitten area. Sucking out the venom yourself isn't effective and may cause more problems. A Sawyer Extraction Pump is the only suction method recommended by most experts. And how many of us keep one of those on hand?
- Call or send someone for help. If you are alone, call for emergency help if you have a mobile phone with you (and it can get reception—this can be a problem in some hiking areas). If you can't make a call from a mobile phone, walk (don't run) to the nearest place you can find a phone or help.

Slithering through life

Snakes are reptiles, which mean they have scales on their bodies, lay eggs, and are cold-blooded. Snakes also have no legs, ears, or eyelids. They can range from 6 inches to $8^1/_2$ feet long and can be found in most habitats throughout the States.

Snakes survive and thrive because they are very effective predators. They have specialized body parts specifically designed to help them catch their favorite prey: rodents. Most people don't know that a snake's tongue, which is usually in constant motion, is really a part of its nose. The snake picks up scent particles with its tongue and then slides it into a special organ, called the *vomeronasal organ* or *Jacobson's organ*, on the roof of its mouth. This organ is connected to the olfactory nerve and the nose.

Another organ that snakes rely on is the heat sensor or pit organ, which is located between the eyes and nose. Members of the pit viper family of snakes (such as rattlesnakes) all have these organs. They use them to "see" an animal's body heat. This is how a pit snake can find and catch its prey in total darkness.

Snakes have no external ears, but they can feel vibrations through their jawbone and body. So they can actually feel someone coming, much as you can feel a train coming by touching the track.

Remember that snakes are among the good guys. If at all possible, encourage them to come to your yard, and you'll have fewer problems with pest species.

SPIDERS

Spiders are amazing creatures; however, some people feel there is nothing more creepy than a spider hovering overhead in its web or scuttling along the floor. There are more than thirty-four thousand different spider species all over the world, and most of them are predaceous! Luckily, most of their victims are insects, which makes spiders a great asset for controlling the numbers of insects in our environment.

Good guys with a bad reputation

Spiders belong to the family of arachnids, and they differ from insects in various ways. All spiders have eight legs and two body segments, whereas all insects have six legs and three body segments. The spider's first body segment, called the *cephalothorax*, has the eyes, venom glands, legs, and fangs. The second segment, called the abdomen, contains the rest of the internal organs, plus the silk glands and spinnerets (from which the spider pulls its silk). Like insects, spiders molt: when the spider outgrows its skin, the old skin splits off to reveal a new one.

Spiders didn't always have a bad reputation. Hundreds of years ago, many people, believing spiders could ward off diseases, ate spiders or wore them around their necks. And today scientists are looking at spider venom as a possible source of new medicines.

Though it's not uncommon to think of webs when one thinks of spiders, not all spiders spin a web. Some spiders use their silk for purposes other than spinning a web to catch their dinner. A few build trap doors or funnels and one species uses its silk as a lasso to catch its prey. Some spiders are hunters that actively run and catch their meals. No matter what method they use to catch their prey, spiders are excellent hunters!

All spiders possess a pair of fangs and venom to help them kill their prey. It is this venom that makes people respect and fear spiders. It should be mentioned, however, that if given a choice, a spider would choose not to bite a human but would save its venom for something it could actually eat!

Potentially dangerous spiders

The three North American spiders that are potentially dangerous to humans are the brown recluse, the black widow, and the new spider on the block, the brown widow. Fortunately, the black widow spider is easily recognized by the distinctive small red hourglass on the underside of its black abdomen. The brown widow looks like the black widow except it is brown and has an orange or yellowish hourglass on its abdomen. Widow spiders build messy webs that resemble cobwebs, in wood piles, garages, and basements. The black widow spider has even been known to build a home in toys left outdoors. You can tell the difference between the webs of widow spiders by looking at the egg cases found in them. The black widow's egg cases are smooth; the brown widow's egg cases have spines sticking out all over. The venom of the widow spiders is very powerful, but generally only a tiny amount is released. In an adult, this usually causes only pain at the site and nausea; however, for a small child the venom can be quite dangerous, and a doctor should be called immediately.

> The average spider eats about one hundred insects a year, and many eat more. In a one-acre field, you might find up to ten thousand spiders. That equals one million insects eaten in one year!

The brown recluse spider is much harder to identify. This very shy spider can be gray or brown and likes to live in warm, dry places. The recluse spider is also called the *sweater drawer spider* and the *violin spider*. The latter name comes from the small violin shape on its back; the former name indicates one of its favorite hiding places—and one spot to watch out for it. Its bite isn't particularly painful—you may even dismiss it as just another spider bite at first. However, soon the flesh next to the bite will start to rot. This process usually isn't painful, but if left untreated, large holes can form in the skin and lead to serious problems.

It's good to know that the brown recluse spider will actually run and hide if it hears you coming. Most bites from the recluse spider occur when the spider is trapped or crushed next to the skin.

 ## SPITTLEBUGS (FROGHOPPERS)

Perhaps you've strolled through your garden or taken a leisurely afternoon hike through a meadow and seen what looks like spit in the branches of plants and grasses. No way are you going to inspect the spit to see what it is! But if you did, you'd see the very bizarre spittlebug or froghopper.

Danger in numbers

These small hopping insects are members of the Cercopidae family. They are greenish to brown in color and have an average length of $1/2$ inch. The adults resemble tiny frogs, with stout heads and bulging eyes, hence the name froghopper. Their other name, spittlebug, comes from the immature nymph's habit of producing a spit-like substance that keeps it from drying out. The adult spittlebug can hop about freely on the plant and fly in search of fresh succulent plants.

Using their piercing-sucking mouth parts, several species of spittlebugs can cause serious damage to plants by stunting their growth. In large numbers, these insects can extract enough of the plant's juices to cause the plant to wilt and die. In the eastern part of the United States, the meadow spittlebug (*Philaenus spumarius*) attacks clover, alfalfa, and strawberries and causes a great deal of economic damage. There are also a couple of species of spittlebugs that damage pine trees. Spittlebugs do the greatest damage in areas that have high humidity.

Controlling the tiny spittlebug is a labor-intensive proposition. One of the best control measures is to cut them out of your plants when you see them. On hardier plants, a very strong stream of water may dislodge the creatures. On heavy crop infestations, one practice is to harvest the crop before the adults can lay their eggs in the late fall, then clean up any grasses or plants around the fields where the adults could lay eggs.

TARANTULA HAWK WASPS

A very large black wasp with red-orange wings and long spiny legs just went whizzing by your head. What on earth could it be doing in your yard? You are hoping it doesn't sting people. Yes, it does sting, but most likely it is looking for a tarantula to feed to its young.

A tarantula's worst nightmare

Tarantula hawks are just one of the species in the spider wasp family (Pompilidae). This family of wasps is highly skilled at catching spiders to feed its developing larvae. Spiders eat both beneficial and pest insects, and the spider wasp's role is to keep the number of spiders in check. However, most gardeners would rather have spiders than insect pests, so it's up to you to decide whether you think spider wasps are beneficial or not.

You don't have to do anything special to attract tarantula hawks to your yard. If you have tarantulas roaming around, then you'll probably have tarantula hawks cruising your yard as well. If one spots a tarantula, the wasp will attack the big spider in its burrow. The wasp will sting the tarantula to paralyze it, and then will deposit an egg on it. The spider remains alive but anesthetized. The wasp's egg will hatch and feed on the live spider until it is ready to spin a cocoon. An adult wasp will emerge from the cocoon to feed on flower pollen and search for more tarantulas.

YELLOW JACKET WASPS

Anyone who has been to a picnic or backyard barbecue that has been invaded by yellow jacket wasps would certainly agree that these insect are pests. However, yellow jacket wasps are beneficial pollinators, predators of insects and spiders, and scavengers on dead animals.

Help to avoid a stinging situation

Wasp traps on the market today claim to keep those pesky dinner invaders at bay. Some are more effective than others; most are based on the principle of attracting the wasps using a bait source, commonly a food attractant.

You can make your own bait using fruit juice (apple is a good choice) and a piece of meat. The trap itself can be made of many things: an old soda bottle, a plastic milk bottle, or even a plastic bag. The idea is to fill the trap container with fruit juice to a depth of about two inches. Then place a small piece of raw meat (like hamburger or fish) in the trap as well. Leave the lid off the bottle and place it out on your picnic table or, even better, on a table all by itself. Ants will also love this trap, but setting it in a pan of water will help deter them.

Now, as the fruit juice ferments and the meat spoils, the trap will give off an odor the wasps should love. The unsuspecting wasps will crawl into the bottle, fall into the juice, and drown. If you use plastic bags, the method is slightly different. First, cut a small hole near the top to allow the wasp to get in. Next, hang the bag, supporting the top in two places (an old wire coat hanger works well) for best results. If you don't want to make your own, you can buy a plastic bag trap similar to this in a garden shop or camping center.

You can use the juice or the meat by itself in the trap, or try various combinations to get just the right bait—one that is irresistible to your neighborhood wasps. If you use meat alone, replace the juice with the same quantity of water; there must be liquid for the wasps to drown in.

Skunks have been known to raid ground wasp nests for wasp larvae. If you know of a ground wasp nest, pour some honey around the nest opening. The honey will attract the neighborhood skunks to the nest, where they can have a meal of honey and wasps.

Insect good guy, but a stinger of humans

Yellow jacket wasps belong to the same wasp family (Vespidae) as hornets and paper wasps. This family of wasps is especially known for its powerful stinger, which the wasp can use over and over again (unlike the honeybee, which can use its stinger only once and then dies).

Paper wasps construct a large nest of many layers of paper, making individual hexagonal cells for the larvae. The wasps construct this nest by chewing wood or foliage, mixing it with their saliva, and then applying the mixture as a sculptor would. Nests are usually found in protected areas like tall trees or house eaves; some are built underground. An average nest may contain from five thousand to twenty-five thousand wasps in the summer. Each nest has a single queen. Unlike bees, most wasp colonies do not live through the winter. The female queen alone overwinters and builds a new nest in the spring.

Adult wasps generally feed on flower nectar and play an important part in pollination for many species of plants. The larvae are fed lots of insects and scavenged pieces of dead animal. It is when the wasps are scavenging for meat to feed their larvae that they become most annoying to humans.

chapter six

Beneficial Insects and Animals

BATS

Bats are one of the most maligned animals of all time. Who doesn't think of a bat when they hear the word "vampire"? Many people still think of bats as dirty bloodsuckers that fly through the night looking for victims. Of course, in the United States people are starting to know better. Here, bats are the heroes of the gardener: they are valuable pollinators, and they also consume large quantities of insects each night. Insect-eating bats usually catch their prey in midair and disappear without a sound, so many people have bats in their yards and probably don't realize they do.

It's great to have a bat about the house

Bats are nocturnal and many are crepuscular, which means they are active at dawn and dusk. They spend their nights searching for food—mostly insects like beetles, moths, leafhoppers, and mosquitoes. A colony of 150 big brown bats can spare farmers in the area from the damage that would be caused by up to eighteen million or more rootworms each summer by eating the rootworm adults and preventing them from laying eggs. Admittedly, bats are indiscriminate feeders that will eat whatever insects they find. We like to think they eat only pest insects, but they will take their share of beneficial insects as well.

One area in which bats excel is mosquito and gnat control. A single little brown bat can catch up to six hundred mosquitoes in one hour. If you have ever been in a cloud of gnats, imagine that cloud ten times worse without bats. In areas with high numbers of mosquitoes, people are now putting up bat houses to encourage bats to roost nearby.

> The twenty million Mexican free-tailed bats that live in Bracken Cave in Texas eat twenty-five tons of insects in a single summer night!

A bat house is easy to make; it resembles a bird house with an entrance in the bottom. There are many plans available for bat houses; the one shown on the following two pages, from Bat Conservation International in Austin, Texas, incorporates simple construction, light weight, and low cost. Smaller bat houses like the one on the following page will be less successful in cool climates.

When you've finished building the house, hang the box at least fifteen to twenty feet off the ground. If building your own bat house is too much trouble, you can order a ready-made house from Bat Conservation International by visiting their website at www.batcon.org.

In addition to eating insects, bats are excellent pollinators, a fact that has been overlooked by many. In rainforest ecosystems, bats play a key role in flower pollination and seed dispersal for many trees and shrubs. Many of the tropical fruit trees grown in the States also depend on bat pollination. Avocados, agave plants (from which tequila is produced), bananas, mangoes, cashews, dates, and figs are just a few plants that benefit from bat pollination.

Bat guano (feces) is also an excellent fertilizer. One study suggests that bat guano will actually reduce pesticide residue in the soil. The bacterium in guano is now being used to detoxify wastes, improve detergents, and produce gasohol and antibiotics.

Sometimes a bat will take up residence in an attic or the eaves of a house. In these cases, the bat becomes an unwanted guest, and screening off that particular area is the best way to send it on its way. Wait for the bat to leave to feed before placing the screening.

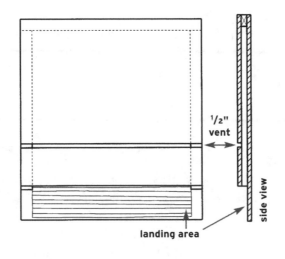

½" vent

side view

landing area

Single-Chamber Bat House (wall mounted)

MATERIALS NEEDED (MAKES 1 HOUSE)

- ¼ sheet (2' x 4') ½" AC, BC or T1-11 (outdoor grade) plywood
- One piece 1" x 2" (³/4" x 1½" finished) x 8' pine (furring strip)
- 20 to 30 exterior-grade screws, 1"
- One pint dark, water-based stain, exterior grade
- One pint water-based primer, exterior grade

- One quart flat, water-based paint or stain, exterior grade
- One tube paintable latex caulk
- 1" x 4" x 28" board for roof (optional, but highly recommended)
- Black asphalt shingles or galvanized metal (optional)
- 6 to 10 roofing nails, ⁷/8" (if using shingles or metal roofing)

RECOMMENDED TOOLS

- Table saw or handsaw
- Variable-speed reversing drill
- Screwdriver bit for drill
- Tape measure or yardstick

- Caulking gun
- Paintbrushes
- Hammer (optional)
- Tin snips (optional)

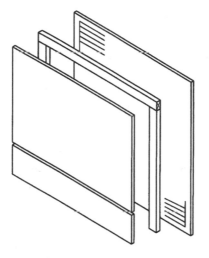

CONSTRUCTION

1. Measure and cut plywood into three pieces: 26$\frac{1}{2}$" x 24," 16$\frac{1}{2}$" x 24," 5" x 24"

2. Roughen inside of backboard and landing area by cutting horizontal grooves with sharp object or saw. Space grooves $\frac{1}{4}$" to $\frac{1}{2}$" apart, cutting $\frac{1}{32}$" to $\frac{1}{16}$" deep.

3. Apply two coats of dark, water-based stain to interior surfaces. Do not use paint, as it will fill grooves.

4. Cut furring strip into one 24" and two 20$\frac{1}{2}$" pieces.

5. Attach furring strips to back, caulking first. Start with 24" piece at top. Roost chamber spacing is $\frac{3}{4}$."

6. Attach front to furring strips, top piece first (caulk first). Leave $\frac{1}{2}$" vent space between top and bottom front pieces.

7. Caulk all outside joints to further seal roost chamber.

8. Attach a 1" x 4" x 28" board to the top as a roof (optional, but highly recommended).

9. Apply three coats of paint or stain to the exterior (use primer for first coat).

10. Cover roof with shingles or galvanized metal (optional).

11. Mount on building (south or east sides usually best).

Reprinted with permission from Bat Conservation International, www.batcon.org

Hanging around with bats

Bats are members of the Chiroptera group of mammals. They are the only true flying mammals, and it's estimated by some experts that they have been flying for about sixty million years. They accomplish this feat by flying with their "hands." The hand of the bat forms the wing. A thin membrane stretches between the finger bones and extends down the hand bones to the forearm, and another membrane attaches the hind legs and tail.

There is some disagreement about bats' eyesight. Most people think bats are blind (hence the old saying, "blind as a bat"). Bats' eyes *are* small, but they aren't blind. However, scientists do agree that bats' vision is probably not needed when they use echolocation (a type of summer night sonar) to locate their food. When bats fly, they emit high-frequency sounds that bounce back from objects around them. Their sensitive ears pick up the sounds, and they can translate these sounds and find their food.

Bats can be found throughout the continental United States. About 40 percent of American bat species are in severe decline, with many listed as threatened or endangered. The little brown bat has a range of just about the entire United States. It is also the world's longest-lived mammal for its size; it has a life span that often exceeds thirty-two years. Most bats are brown to black in color, and all hang with their heads down when at rest.

Some bats migrate; others do not. Those bats that do not migrate hibernate in their roosts. There, they go into torpor for the winter (unlike hummingbirds, which go into torpor each and every night!). Most bat litters consist of one or two young per year, which are born in May or June. This slow reproduction rate makes the bat exceptionally vulnerable to extinction. The young, called pups, stay with their mothers for about a month, by which time they are able to fly and feed themselves.

Hands off

Though all mammals can contract rabies, it's the reporting of rabid bats that often makes the evening news. The estimated number of bats that actually contract rabies is less than 0.5 percent of all bats. Even though this number is very small, it should still serve as a warning to never pick up a bat off the ground. Grounded bats are usually sick or injured and will not appreciate being picked up. If you do find a grounded bat that must be moved or disposed of, use a shovel to pick it up. Place the bat in a bucket or a hard-sided box with a lid. (Bats can bite through a plastic bag.) Many areas require you to report grounded bats, so contact the agriculture officials in your area for advice.

BEES

Everyone knows how beneficial bees are in pollinating fruit, vegetables, and flowers. Although many of us have great respect for the job the honeybee does, most of us are still afraid of the bee's sting.

The truth about Africanized bees

Reports of the potential threat of the Africanized honeybee ("killer bee") increased the fear of bees in the United States. But in fact, African bees are great pollinators and can survive well in arid conditions, and states that have African bees have found their reputation for being extremely aggressive to be exaggerated.

- Africanized bees can breed with European bees and produce a hive that has the traits and aggression of the dominant original African bees. These hives are referred to as *Africanized.*

- Africanized bees are only slightly smaller than the ordinary European honeybees we commonly see. To most people, the bees look identical.

- An individual Africanized honeybee flying or pollinating a flower will not pose a threat to people.

- Africanized bees are most defensive when disturbed or provoked near their hive. The vibration of a lawn mower near their hive can disturb the bees and cause them to swarm defensively.

- Africanized bees are ten times more likely to sting than European honeybees, but like the European bees they can sting only once before dying.

- Africanized honeybee venom is no more toxic than European honeybee venom.

- Eliminating nesting sites on your property can reduce bee problems.
- You can possibly outrun an Africanized bee attack if you sprint at full speed (fifteen mph) for an eighth to a quarter of a mile.
- It has been estimated that it would take about 1,100 bee stings to kill an average adult.
- To reduce your chance of an attack, wear light-colored clothing and avoid perfumes around possible Africanized nests.
- If you are attacked, cover your head and move inside a building or car immediately.

Keeping bees in their place

Africanized honeybees have expanded their territory by an average of two hundred miles per year since their unfortunate escape from a Brazilian test site in 1957. The bees expand their range by swarming. When a hive is getting crowded, it sends a signal to the workers to produce a new queen. She and a large number of the workers leave the old hive to establish a new one. During the swarm, scout bees are on the lookout for a suitable new hive site. European bees also swarm, but Africanized bees swarm more frequently because their hives are smaller and reach capacity more quickly. Swarming bees have gorged themselves with honey in advance of the move, so they are not dangerous.

Another difference between European and Africanized honeybees is that Africanized bees will establish a hive in the ground, whereas European bees prefer a raised hive. This habit of ground hives requires us to be on the alert. The simple act of mowing the lawn near a hive can send an Africanized colony into a frenzy. In areas where Africanized bees are known to be resident, all of us, particularly parents of young children, need to check our property carefully for potential ground hive sites and destroy them. Any opening bigger than one inch is a potential hive; for example, old burrows (from rabbits or other animals) can be taken over by the bees. In Arizona, meter readers have to be extremely

> Bees make sixty thousand nectar-collecting trips to flowers to produce just one teaspoon of honey!

careful when removing meter plates, because Africanized hives have been found in several meter boxes.

Africanized bees are excellent honey producers, even in times of poor flower production, and it was once thought that cross-breeding the less aggressive European bees with the Africanized bee would produce a bee that would be a superior honey producer.

A honey of a deal

Humans have been robbing bees of their sweet irresistible honey for all of recorded nectar-collecting history. In Spain, rock paintings that depict honey gathering have been found, dating back to 7000 BCE. The art of modern beekeeping has come a long way since then: today, honeybees can be found and kept in most areas of the world, except the polar regions.

Most people do not realize that prior to 1500 the common honeybee (*Apis mellifera*) lived only in the Old World: Europe, Africa, and Asia. As new lands were colonized, settlers brought along many of their favorite animals, like horses and bees. The first record of bees being established in North America was in 1638. Our native North American bees do not produce the elaborate hives of the European bees, nor do they have the honey-producing potential.

Bees were first brought to the New World to produce honey and wax. It wasn't until this century that the bee's importance as a pollinator was appreciated. In California alone, forty-two different nut, fruit, vegetable, forage, and seed crops, with an estimated annual revenue of $1.5 billion, rely directly on bee pollination. Even the world's most important forage crop for animals, alfalfa, depends on cross-pollination by bees.

GREEN LACEWINGS

Gardeners have long enjoyed having green lacewings in their gardens. Many have marveled at their beauty and grace, not knowing it's the *larvae* of this insect that are great to have around.

A lion of a predator

Those delicate-looking insects are definitely wolves in sheep's clothing. The larval form is a fierce-looking, voracious aphid predator, aptly nick-named the "aphid lion." Though it also eats mites, mealybugs, and other small insects, its primary target is aphids. The aphid lion almost appears to be a cross between an earwig (both have large mandibles) and a lady-bird beetle larva (both have large spiny abdomens). The lacewing larva first uses its large mandibles like tongs to grab its prey; next, the mandibles do double duty and suck the juices from the victim.

If you think this illustration paints an ugly picture of these larvae, you are right. Many a new gardener has killed this larval insect because it looks like it must be harmful. Some gardeners say they look like alligators, with sickle-like mouth parts. Lace-wing larvae have even been known to place the dried bodies of their victims on top of their own bodies as camouflage, to be better able to sneak up on their prey.

Lacewing eggs can be purchased by mail order, or sometimes large nurseries will order them for you. A short list of suppliers can be found in the Resources and Buying Guide section at the end of this book.

A delicate life?

The lacewing belongs to the order of insects called Neuroptera (meaning nerve wing). Adult lacewings have four beautifully clear, delicate wings, all equal in size. Lacewings have veins resembling fine lace crisscrossing through their wings, hence their name. When at rest, this insect holds its wings roof-like over its body.

The adults range in size from $1/2$ to $3/4$ inch long and have striking golden eyes. There are brown as well as green lacewings, and their larval form is also predaceous. Adult lacewings are not predators; they feed on honeydew from aphids as well as pollen and nectar from plants.

Lacewings can be found in many types of vegetation, including grasses, trees, and shrubs. They will search out aphid colonies and lay their eggs among them. Lacewing females lay their eggs on long, thin stalks on the underside of leaves, because otherwise the first larvae to hatch would cannibalize the other eggs upon hatching. This way the newly hatched larva eats the stalk, giving the rest of the eggs a chance to hatch.

Be aware that, as beautiful as lacewings are, they can give off a very unpleasant odor if handled or disturbed.

GROUND BEETLES (CARABID BEETLES)

Ground beetles, which range in length from $1/4$ to 1 inch, are great nocturnal predators that like to hide under logs, stones, bark, and soil in the daytime. They are usually black and shiny, but some can be marked by bright colors. Most gardeners don't know how good these little beetles are for pest control.

How good are they?

Both the adult carabids and the larvae are excellent predators. Another name for this beneficial beetle is the predaceous ground beetle. Some of their favorite insect meals are cutworms, grubs, root maggots, and other soft-bodied pests found both above and below the soil. Some species of ground beetles love to feed on slugs and snails as well. When these beetles are disturbed, they will run quickly; rarely, they will fly.

To ensure a good supply of ground beetles in your garden, provide a place for them to hide. Place a board or log in a spot near your garden or between your plants. The board should be placed on bare soil where it isn't in direct sun all day, as the beetles like a dark and moist area. Check the hiding place often to see whether you do indeed have ground beetles working for you. Providing a hiding place sometimes encourages other pest species (such as snails and slugs) to congregate there, but the beetles should be happy to have a meal deliver itself.

Knowing the good guy

Ground beetles belong to the Carabidae family—with 2,500 species, the second largest family of beetles in North America. With the sheer numbers of beetles in the world—about a quarter of a million species known so far, and about twenty-nine thousand species just in North America—how do you tell if you have a predaceous ground beetle and not a potential pest in your garden?

To identify what type of beetle you have, first catch one in a jar. By looking closely at the antennae and wing covers with a small magnifying lens, you can distinguish predaceous ground beetles from other beetles. The antenna segments of the ground beetle will all be the same length, and the antennae themselves will be attached on the sides of the beetle's head between the eye and the mandible or jaw. Most ground beetles will also have longitudinal grooves or rows of punctures on their wing covers (called *elytra*).

One well-known ground beetle, the caterpillar hunter, was imported from Europe to fight the gypsy moth, a notorious tree pest. But beware— this brightly colored green and blue beetle gives off an offensive odor when handled.

HOVER FLIES (SYRPHID FLIES)

You see little flying insect "helicopters" all over your flowers—they seem to hover motionless, resembling small hairless bees. What could they be, and what are they doing in your yard?

Flower flies

This interesting fly is one of the gardener's greatest allies. The hover fly (called the *flower fly* by many) belongs to the fly family Syrphidae, one of the largest families, with 940 species in North America. Many of these flies are brightly colored and resemble various types of bees, wasps, and bumble- bees. Though they look like insects that are capable of stinging, hover flies are harmless to people. Because they mimic stinging insects, many other predators (including birds) will leave them alone.

To know for sure whether you have hover flies or bees, check the number of wings. Hover flies are true flies and have only two wings, whereas bees have four wings. Many hover flies also have an abdomen that is flattened from top to bottom, unlike true bees, which have a very round abdomen.

The adult hover fly feeds on flower nectar, which makes it an excellent pollinator and a great asset to every garden. An added bonus is that the larvae of some hover fly species are great predators as well. One of their favorite types of prey is aphids, although they also like mealybugs and other small insects. The worm-like larvae possess large fangs that they use to grab their prey and drain the fluids from their bodies, in much the same way that lacewing larvae do.

Female hover flies will lay their eggs right in the midst of an aphid colony. When it comes to aphid control, only the ladybird beetle larva (or aphid lion) is more effective than the hover fly larva. In some hover fly species, the larvae are scavengers that live in the nests of ants, bees, and wasps.

Laying out the welcome mat

To ensure that hover flies flock to your garden, plant plenty of nectar-rich flowers, which the adults love. Border plantings of daisies, sunflowers, marigolds, and an assortment of your area's native flowers will ensure that hover flies keep visiting your garden for the entire season.

HUMMINGBIRDS

Long before the common honeybee was imported into this country from Europe, hummingbirds were hard at work pollinating flowers here. These small dynamos must visit approximately one thousand of their favored flowers to supply the calories they need each day to survive. Each hummingbird will consume more than half its total weight in food each day, and a big part of that will be insects. The insects provide protein, minerals, vitamins, and fats, which are essential nutrients for the birds.

The life of a hummingbird

Hummingbirds, those small jewels at your feeder, are some of the world's most intriguing birds. They hold many records of the bird world, including these:

- One species is the smallest bird in the world. The bee hummingbird weighs only 0.09 ounces!

- They are the only birds whose wings beat in a figure-eight pattern, allowing them to hover and fly backward rapidly. The smaller species (there are 342 hummingbird species worldwide) have an average wing beat of eighty beats per second and up to two hundred beats per second during courtship displays.
- At night, hummingbirds regularly go into a form of hibernation called torpor. Chilean hummers were once called "resurrection birds" because they appeared to rise from the dead each morning.
- They have the highest normal body temperature of any bird, up to a whopping 106°Fahrenheit.
- Their hearts are the biggest in relation to their body size of all warm-blooded animals. Their heart rate can reach 1,260 beats per minute.

Inviting hummingbirds to your garden

Making your yard an attractive place for hummingbirds to visit is simple and rewarding. Plant flowering shrubs and vines that produce lots of nectar. In the western United States, there are about 130 species of plants, like the cape honeysuckle and trumpet vines, that exhibit some adaptation for hummingbirds.

Hang a hummingbird feeder. San Diego Zoo hummingbird keepers recommend skipping the commercial sugar solutions and filling your feeder with this simple, inexpensive recipe (see page 121).

Zookeepers avoid putting red food coloring in the water. It is unknown how the coloring affects the birds, so it's better to leave it out. Instead, buy a red feeder, one with a red tip, or one with a design of red flowers on the bottle (you can also paint the flowers on yourself). Put in only the amount of sugar water that the hummers will consume in two to four days to prevent mold from growing in your feeder and to keep the sugar solution from turning rancid. If mold does grow, use toothpaste on a bottlebrush to clean inside the bottle or in hard-to-reach areas. A tablespoon of rice shaken inside when cleaning will also help remove mold.

Keeping ants off your feeder

Now that you have hummingbirds coming to your yard, you may find that ants are flocking to the sweet solution as well. Here are some simple and effective methods for controlling ants:

- Make a moat on the feeder's suspending wire. Punch a hole in a jar lid or bottle cap and place the cap on the wire about halfway down. Use a bit of silicone glue underneath the cap to hold it in place and make it waterproof. Just fill the cap with water (or even mentholated rub) and you have a barrier moat for your feeder.

- A sticky string is another option. Tie a strong piece of string to the feeder's suspending wire, so that when the feeder is hung it will hang down an extra four or five inches. After you hang the feeder, smear Tanglefoot (which you can buy at any garden shop) on the string. It is extremely sticky, so be careful.

- Hot pepper, such as hot sauce or cayenne pepper, can also be applied to the suspending string to help keep ants away.

- Oil of eucalyptus applied to a suspending string is also an excellent way of repelling ants. If you can't find oil of eucalyptus, use mentholated rub instead.

- Hang your hummingbird feeder inside the supports of a hanging plant. Any dripping sugar water falls into the plant and not onto the ground, which would attract ants.

Sugar Solution for Hummingbirds

1 cup warm water
1/4 cup white sugar (do not use brown sugar or honey)

Stir the water and sugar together until the sugar is dissolved, and immediately use in your feeder.

LADYBUGS (LADYBIRD BEETLES)

Who doesn't know of this aphid-eating beetle, which children tell to "fly away home"? The beginning to this old medieval nursery rhyme tells ladybugs to fly away so farmers could burn old hop-vines in the fields in preparation for another planting. Even then farmers knew the benefits of ladybugs.

The ultimate beneficial insect

Except for two species—the Mexican bean beetle and the squash beetle—all the members of this family of beetles are beneficial. There are about five thousand different species of ladybugs worldwide and four hundred in North America. They belong to the beetle family Coccinellidae, which means "little red sphere." However, ladybugs come in other colors beside red, such as orange, pink, yellow, and black. Their bright colors serve as a warning sign to birds and other potential predators that they don't taste good. If attacked by a predator, ladybugs ooze a foul-smelling yellow liquid from their leg joints. This liquid is actually their blood, and a taste of it is all it takes to convince their attacker not to continue snacking on them! Ladybugs can have as many as twenty spots on their wing coverings, and some species have no spots.

The larval stage of the ladybug does not look anything like the beautiful adult stage; in fact, they are often assumed to be pests. However, they are great predators that can consume large quantities of aphids, one of their preferred foods. Both the adults and the larvae will feed together on a colony of aphids or other insect pests. The size and coloration of the larval stages vary among the species, but generally the larvae are soft bodied and shaped like a miniature alligator. Newly hatched larvae are less than an eighth of an inch long. As they grow, they reach about one half inch long. The larvae can be gray, black, or blue with bright yellow or orange markings on the body, but the black body with yellow/orange markings are the most common form recognized.

Ladybug females will lay up to one thousand eggs, and populations can build up quickly. The adults eat not only insects but also pollen and nectar.

Ladybug species live from one to two years, and in the winter, the adults of many species will hibernate. They look for spaces under bark, in crevices, or under house eaves and often congregate by the thousands, making quite an impressive sight.

Ladybugs' revered namesake

Ladybugs are also called lady bird or lady beetles. Legend has it that in Europe during the Middle Ages, swarms of insects were destroying crops. The farmers, after trying everything they could to stop the destructive insects, prayed to the Virgin Mary for help. Not long afterward, swarms of ladybugs descended on the fields and ate up the destroying insects, thus saving the crops. The farmers called these insects "The Beetles of Our Lady," and today we know them as ladybugs.

Ladybugs to the rescue

In the 1880s, California's citrus growers were faced with fighting the destructive insect cottony-cushion scale from Australia. It was killing and stunting large groves of lemon and orange trees. The growers decided to put the ladybugs and their voracious appetites to the ultimate test. They bought $1,500 worth of Australian ladybugs (called vedalia beetles) and released them into the orchards. Within two years, the scale infestation was controlled and the trees began to bear fruit again. The ladybugs had saved an entire industry, which today is worth half a billion dollars.

Since then, numerous species of ladybugs have been "employed" around the world to help control outbreaks of crop-destroying pests. The convergent ladybug, however, is undoubtedly the "aphid-eating champ" of all the ladybug species. It is named for the two converging white dashes on the black thorax portion of its body. This ladybug has been commonly used by many orchard owners, plant nurseries, farmers, and homeowners for pest control since 1910. These ladybugs can be purchased during the spring and summer months at your local nursery or garden center for use in your own backyard when you see an aphid or another soft-bodied pest population climbing. If you don't have pests in your garden, however, don't purchase ladybugs thinking you will prevent an infestation. Ladybugs won't stay on your plants if they don't have anything to eat. Instead, keep them in mind as part of your integrated pest management plan.

How to release ladybugs in your yard

Gardeners often report that, when they release ladybugs into their gardens, the first thing the ladybugs do is fly away. Actually, this a natural first response to being released. To keep them from all flying away, try wetting the foliage where you have aphids or other pests you want controlled. The ladybugs are thirsty and hungry when first released, so offering them a drink and the food (pests) that are available will encourage them to stay around. Release the ladybugs on the damp leaves early in the morning or in the evening. Never release them in the heat of the day.

A symbol of good luck

Many cultures believe ladybugs are good luck and forecasters of good things to come. In the past, it was believed not only that ladybugs brought good luck, but also that killing a ladybug brought a person sadness and misfortune. Some of the old legends are quite fascinating:

- The French believed if a ladybug landed on you, it would take whatever ailment you had with it when it flew away.
- The Swiss told their children they were brought to them by ladybugs.
- In Belgium, if a ladybug crawled across a maiden's hand, it was believed that she would marry within a year.
- In some Asian cultures, it was believed that ladybugs understood human language and were blessed by God.
- British farmers believed if they saw numerous ladybugs flying around in spring, the harvest that year would be bountiful.
- American pioneers considered it a good omen if they found a ladybug in their house during winter.

LIZARDS

People who are repelled by snakes may find lizards almost as repulsive. But lizards, just like snakes, are great predators. No self-respecting lizard could pass up a tasty insect meal. So before you shoo that lizard away from your garden, encourage it to hang around for a meal.

The benefits of having a lizard around

Most lizards are diurnal, meaning they are awake in the daytime and asleep at night. Many of our most dreaded pests are also diurnal, so try using the following tricks to encourage that lizard you saw prowling around your garden to look for a meal when pests are most active.

Most lizards prefer to live in grassy cover, and a completely well-manicured yard won't provide much shelter for them. A small "wild" patch of herbs or flowers will give lizards the shelter they need. Lizards also use secluded areas to wait for their prey. Rock walls are a favorite spot. They provide cover and a warm place to bask. You can encourage lizards to stay in your garden by providing them with some shelter. Small clay pots or an old wooden box, turned upside down and propped up on one side with a small stone in the corner of your yard, can provide a good hiding place for a lizard.

If you are lucky enough to have an alligator lizard in your yard, you probably don't have any black widow spiders. Alligator lizards will climb bushes and shrubs, or prowl dark basements and garages, in search of this delicious prey. In the absence of black widows, this lizard is also known to feed on almost any small animal that it can catch and swallow.

The lives of lizards

Lizards belong to the largest living group of reptiles and date back to the Triassic Period. There are 115 different species of lizards in North America and 3,000 species worldwide.

Lizards come in many shapes, sizes, and colors. Some lizards don't even look like lizards, but instead look like snakes. The only way to tell a legless lizard from a snake is to look at its eyes. Legless lizards have movable eyelids, whereas snakes do not.

Many people confuse lizards with salamanders. Lizards have scales and claws, and they lay eggs on land. Salamanders, on the other hand, are amphibians; they have moist skin and no scales or claws, and they spend part of their lives (the egg stage) in water. But salamanders, like lizards, are carnivores that are great to have around for garden pest control.

The smallest lizard is a gecko that is less than three inches long when grown, and the largest is the Komodo dragon, native to a range of small islands in Indonesia, which can reach a length of ten feet and weigh up to three hundred pounds.

Not all lizards are strictly meat eaters. Many lizards also eat plants, but damage to garden plants done by lizards is usually minimal, if it happens at all. When the weather gets cold, lizards don't congregate in dens, as many snakes do. Instead, they usually hibernate alone in cracks and crevices. In the spring, you will again see the lizards sunning themselves on rocks and fences.

There are only two lizards that are venomous—the Gila monster of the southwestern United States and Mexico's beaded lizard. They do not have fangs, as snakes do, but instead have grooves in their back teeth. When venomous lizards bite, they hold on until the venom runs down the grooves in their teeth and into the wound. They are pretty slow moving and generally do not pose much danger to humans.

 ## NEMATODES

Nematodes are minute nonsegmented worms that are pointed on both ends. Many nematodes are parasitic and, when added to the soil, will seek out and destroy pests, including fleas, cutworms, and beetle grubs. However, some nematodes are also plant parasites that cause plant diseases.

Insect assassins

As beneficial as some nematodes are, there are others that are equally destructive. Those nematodes that are plant parasites attack plant roots, causing damage to the root, which prevents the plant from getting the water and nutrients it needs to grow. Don't be surprised if you go to a nursery looking for beneficial nematodes and get surprised looks in return. Some plant nematodes are major pests, and news of beneficial nematodes is slow to circulate.

Certain nematode species also are parasitic to animals. Canine heartworms, hookworms, and pinworms are a few common animal nematode parasites.

Beneficial nematodes are those that are known to attack specific organisms. The nematode that is specific for fleas attacks only fleas, so you don't have to worry that it will attack something else in your garden. It has been estimated that soil-dwelling nematodes have the potential to kill more than four hundred different kinds of borer and soil-dwelling pests.

When a nematode enters a host, it releases a bacterium that slowly kills the host. The nematode needs the host to complete its life cycle. The offspring that are produced then go out and search for a new host. If all the host species are gone, the nematodes will die.

The common species of nematodes commercially sold for garden application, Sc (*Steinernema carpocapsae*) and Hb (*Heterorhabditis bacteriophora*), are usually available in the spring. There are various strains of each, and your local nursery personnel should know which ones are effective in your area and for your problem. The nematodes that target fleas can also be found in many pet supply outlets.

Nematodes are most effective in the first two to three weeks after application. The nematodes will continue to control pests after that, but they need a moist soil environment in which to live, so reapplication may be necessary if the soil dries out too much and pests are still present.

Follow directions carefully when applying the nematodes to the soil. You don't want to expose them to direct sunlight, so it's best to apply them in the late evening after the soil has been moistened. This gives the nematodes the best chance to get into the soil and do the job you want them to do. Also, try not to mix different types of nematodes together in the same area at the same time. Some nematode species don't live well together.

PARASITIC WASPS

Most parasitic wasps are quite tiny and therefore are generally not noticed by humans, but the job they do killing pests is nothing less than monumental.

Small wonders

The wasp does its killing by laying its eggs on the eggs and larvae of a target host. The eggs of the wasp hatch and start feeding on the host. Some parasitic wasps larvae feed on the outside of the host, whereas others bore into the host and feed from the inside. The host slowly dies as the immature larval wasp matures.

Most parasitic wasps belong to one of these insect superfamilies: Ichneumonidae, Braconidae, Chalcidoidea, and Proctotrupoidea.

Many of these tiny wasps are commercially available. They are usually shipped as pupae in parasitized hosts, ready to be distributed among your plants, where they will emerge as adults and search for hosts on which to lay their eggs.

Here are some of the more important parasitic wasps:

- The whitefly parasite (*Encarsia formosa*) lays its eggs in the scale-like nymph stage of the whitefly, causing the scale to blacken as the wasps develop and eat the host from the inside. It is recommended that you release these wasps in warm weather, at a rate of two to five wasps per square foot of garden. It's best to release the wasps weekly over a two-month period.

- Trichogramma wasps are extremely tiny wasps that are of great benefit to the gardener. One species, *Trichogramma pretiosum*, will seek out and parasitize the eggs of about two hundred different kinds of butterflies and moths. Other species of *Trichogramma* wasps are a bit more specific in their selection of hosts. Most experts recommend one wasp for every foot of garden. It is best to release the wasps at the time when most host species lay their eggs. Your neighborhood nursery or county agriculture department will have the correct information for your area.

- The pedio wasp (*Pediobius foveolatus*), or bean beetle parasite, is an excellent addition in the fight against Mexican bean beetles. This wasp targets the beetle's larval stage.

Most of the parasitic wasps that are commercially available will be found for sale at nurseries and garden supply outlets, or you can buy them directly from a supplier. Directions for best results usually come with the purchased wasps, but you should also ask other gardeners or professionals in your area which wasps work best for them and under what conditions. A list of commercial suppliers dealing in beneficial insects can be found in the Resources and Buying Guide in the back of this book.

PRAYING MANTISES

Generally, when people think of insects that are great to have around the garden, they think of the praying mantis. Those fascinating large green insects seem to understand every word you say to them. (Or at least they turn their heads as if they're listening!)

Its benefits are just so-so

Unfortunately, the lovely insect that we have come to admire for its beneficial qualities rates only poor to average in pest control. They are indeed predators, but they'll eat any insect they find, whether that insect is beneficial or a pest. (They'll even eat each other.) All an insect has to do is pass within reach to become the mantis's lunch.

Many gardeners have purchased praying mantises and introduced them into their gardens. They usually arrive as egg cases, and the hope is that the praying mantises will hatch and keep pest populations down. Unfortunately, the nymphs have a low survival rate, and few develop into adults.

Praying or preying?

Praying mantises got their name from the way they wait for their prey. Because they sit perfectly still with their front legs upraised, people thought they looked like they were praying.

Praying mantises belong to the insect family Mantidae and are cousins of the walking sticks and crickets. These slow-moving insects are usually green to brown in color and can range up to five inches in length, though in the States the average length is two to three inches. Mantises are chiefly tropical insects, but they have been successfully introduced to cooler climates.

The distinctive front legs of the mantis are armed with strong spines that can snap back firmly to hold onto prey. The mantis is a voracious eater, and the female will consume the male after mating. Interestingly, the mantis is the only insect that can turn its head and look backward. Other insects must turn their entire body to look behind them.

Mantises overwinter as eggs, with two hundred or more packed in an egg case (ootheca) that is laid in the grass or on twigs. The young hatch in early summer and start looking for anything to eat—usually their own brothers and sisters. Mantises, which have only one generation per year, usually reach full maturity in early fall.

ROBBER FLIES

Have you ever been out in your yard and seen a large bee swoop out of nowhere, grab another insect, and fly off? No, you weren't seeing things. Some robber flies look like bees, and most prey on other insects.

A wolf in sheep's clothing

What better way to get close to your prey than by appearing to be a harmless neighbor? That's just what robber flies love to do. They lie in wait and then dart out and grab their victims in midair—hence, their name.

Robber flies belong to the fly family Asilidae, which includes over 850 different North American species. They are predaceous in both the larval form and the adult form. As larvae, they live underground or in decaying wood and feed primarily on the eggs and larvae of beetles and other insects. It's as adults that robber flies do their best insect control. They will feed on just about any insect they can catch, from bees to dragonflies.

Robber flies have many guises. They range from $^1/_4$ to $1^1/_4$ inches in length and resemble flies, bees, and wasps. All of them have bulging eyes with a dent in between, two wings, antennae that project prominently forward, and a long proboscis, which they use to stab their victims. Most robber flies have a very long and pointed abdomen, but this isn't seen in the species of robber flies that resemble bees. They also make a very loud buzzing sound when they fly, sounding almost like a bee that needs a tune-up!

Inviting them home

Good news—you really don't have to do anything special to encourage robber flies to visit your garden. If you have insects in your yard, then chances are you'll have robber flies looking for a meal.

Robber flies are especially good at making meals of flying insects. They are fast fliers and prefer to catch their prey on the wing. Sometimes the robber fly will sit motionless in a tall plant or tree and wait for a victim to fly into range. The robber fly will then dart out and grab the insect with its long legs, which are specially designed with spurs on the inside to hold the prey. These flies will actually attack insects as large as or sometimes even larger than themselves. Robber flies can be found in just about any habitat, even at the tops of giant sequoia trees. Because of their great flying skills, you probably won't see robber flies stopping to eat aphids from a leaf—even though many of us wish they would!

TOADS AND FROGS

Last time your children brought you a toad they found in your yard, what did you do? Have them drop it over the fence into your neighbor's yard? Next time, think twice, because that little toad is a giant asset to your garden.

Calling all toads (and frogs)

Toads and frogs are truly insect-eating machines. No insect is safe from the lightning-fast tongues of these amphibians. One toad or frog in your garden can go a long way toward keeping insects under control.

A toad isn't just a sometime carnivore. Some predators will start nibbling on your garden vegetables when their favorite food supply is exhausted, but toads won't. If the toad's food supply disappears (a rare occurrence, but it happens), the toad will move on and look for insects elsewhere. But with a bit of planning, you can make toads, and even frogs, permanent guests in your yard.

All amphibians need water to complete their life cycles. Frogs are much more dependent on water than toads are and will require a garden pond to take up residency in your yard. A toad, however, will survive nicely with some shelter and a large clay saucer full of water. The shelter can be made of anything that will provide a fairly damp environment. A small cave in a rock garden (or just a broken clay pot turned upside down) can provide an excellent home for a toad. Just make sure the opening is big enough for the toad and sheltered from the wind.

> One lowly toad can eat between ten thousand and twenty thousand slugs, flies, grubs, cutworms, or grasshoppers (or any other insect you can name) per year!

Toads and frogs are very susceptible to pesticide poisoning, so be extremely careful with any toxic products near the toad's or frog's home or pond.

Don't kiss too many frogs

An old wives' tale tells of getting warts from handling frogs and toads. Most people know this isn't true, but they don't know that some toads and frogs secrete a toxin from their skin that can be very irritating.

chapter seven

Beneficial Plants and All-Purpose Repellents

INSECT-REPELLING PLANTS

Our ancestors routinely used companion plants for more effective gardening. Before the invention of chemical pesticides, the art of using companion plants to confuse, repel, or attract insects was relied upon for successful food production. Most gardeners today know very little of the garden practices of long ago, and some of this lost knowledge could be beneficial to both the gardener and the environment.

The benefits of companion plants become obvious when you see the number of pests decrease, but the ways in which companion plants keep pests away are as varied as the plants themselves. Here are some of the ways companion plantings protect your garden vegetables:

- By producing an odor that masks or hides your garden from a pest
- By producing an odor that repels a pest

- As a trap plant that attracts the pest, so it can be easily removed from your garden
- As a perfect breeding ground for beneficial insects, by providing food and/or shelter

Ornamental flowers and garden plants

Many of us are familiar with the repellent quality of marigolds. Beneficial insects need a constant food source in your garden, and many flowering plants, including marigolds, produce numerous flowers rich in pollen and nectar for the entire growing season. Various other flowers and garden plants have also been found to be helpful to the gardener, and many of these have been mentioned in other sections of this book. Here are some popular companion plantings you can try:

- Grown with carrots, onions can help control destructive nematodes.
- Growing horseradish with potatoes helps repel Colorado potato beetles.
- Catnip planted near eggplant deters flea beetles.
- Planting tomatoes or parsley with asparagus helps control asparagus beetles.
- Parsley gone to flower makes a great attractant and food source for the beneficial braconid wasp.
- Nasturtiums planted as a border can help deter whiteflies and squash bugs.
- Nasturtiums are a favorite of aphids, and planting them near your garden will provide a trap plant for aphids.
- Allow a few of your radishes or broccoli to go to flower—these blossoms make a great attractant for many beneficial insects.
- Our friend the marigold, planted in vegetable gardens, produces a scent that repels many garden pests. Some marigolds, like the beautiful lemon-scented marigold, are loved by beneficial insects.
- Mint is said to repel mosquitoes and also produces an odor that many cabbage pests and aphids dislike.
- Spearmint is a favorite of beneficial insects.

- Rue, carefully planted (some people are allergic to it), is known to repel Japanese beetles.

- Many beneficial insects love buckwheat, so plant some if you have the room.

- Tansy has a long history of repelling cucumber beetles, Japanese beetles, squash beetles, and even ants. However, use tansy only in a garden without cabbage, because cabbage worms love it. Tansy is also a favorite of many beneficial insects.

- Cosmos planted around the garden can attract many beneficial insects.

- Early-flowering plants such as gazanias and calendulas will help beneficials get established in your garden early, so they'll be ready for any pests that try to move in.

- Yarrow produces a lot of pollen and nectar and is prized by many beneficials, such as bees and wasps.

- Ladybird beetles love morning glory and goldenrod.

- Many species of candytuft will attract beneficial syrphid flies.

Herbs

Herb planting to control unwanted pests has an extra advantage, because when it's time to harvest the crop you've protected with the herbs, you can harvest the herbs, too. They can be used fresh in cooking or dried for later use. Here are some excellent companion plantings using herbs:

- Planting basil alongside your tomatoes helps control tomato hornworms.

- Thyme planted with cabbage helps control flea beetles, cabbage worms, and white cabbage butterflies.

- Dill is great to plant not only for its herb quality, but because beneficial insects like it for its pollen and nectar.

- Fennel is a favorite of many beneficial insects.

- Anise planted in your yard will give off a lovely licorice smell (and attract parasitic wasps, too).

ANIMAL-REPELLING PLANTS

Gopher Plants

Maybe you've heard of this wonderful plant, which, when planted in and around a garden, repels gophers and other animals such as rabbits and moles like mad. What is it, and how does it work?

PLANTS TO THE RESCUE

The gopher or mole plant (*Euphorbia lathyris*) is a member of a very diverse group of plants. Euphorbias can be shrubs, perennials, biennials, annuals, or succulents. Most have milky sap that tastes and smells very unpleasant. Some are poisonous and quite irritating to the skin. Most euphorbia flowers are a group of colored bracts, not true flowers. The true flowers are usually inside the bracts and are very inconspicuous.

Legend claims that the gopher plant's sap is so poisonous and irritating that gophers and moles can't stand to be anywhere near it. However, test trials indicate mixed results from the plant. But if you happen to be one of those for whom the plant works, that's great. Plant it around your garden for gopher protection. The sap is indeed poisonous, so be careful about planting it where it can be reached by small children and chewing pets.

GOPHER IT!

The gopher plant, which grows well from seed, should be planted in an area that gets full sun. The plant is a biennial and will reach its full height of five feet by the second year. It grows as a tall single stem with long, narrow pointed leaves growing at right angles to the stem. During the second year, it will set a cluster of yellow flowers at the top of the stem. When the flowers set seed, the plant will die. Most nurseries either carry gopher plant seeds or can order them for you.

ALL-PURPOSE REPELLENTS

Chiles

Chiles can be one of a gardener's greatest allies. Depending on the type of pest that is bothering your garden, chiles prepared in many different forms can be just what the doctor ordered.

Chiles are members of the Capsicum plant family, which has over two hundred different varieties. They have been traced as far back as 6200 BCE in Peru. Christopher Columbus even got into the act when he first found chiles and thought they were peppers—hence the common name of chile peppers. But chiles are not peppers at all—true peppers are what we use in our pepper mills.

When using chiles for repellents, you need to use *hot* chiles. Chiles are rated under a system called Scoville Heat Units. The higher the number in the rating system, the hotter the chile. For example, common bell peppers rate 0, jalapeños rate 3,500 to 4,500 units, tabascos rate 30,000 to 50,000 units, and habaneros rate a whopping 200,000 to 300,000 units. The units rate the heat produced by the compound capsaicin, which is inside the ribs of the chile. Generally, the smaller the chile, the higher the heat units.

Chiles are easy to grow, and it's a good idea to grow a few plants for that special repellent cocktail you'll be making for the uninvited "guests" that keep dropping by. Chiles grow into nice bushy plants, usually $1^{1}/_{2}$ to 2 feet tall. They look beautiful as a low hedge or in containers. Chile plants are easy to find in your local nursery, but if you are looking for a particularly hot variety, chances are you will have to order seeds. If your nursery can't order them for you, check out *The Whole Chile Pepper Book* by Dave DeWitt and Nancy Gerlach (Little, Brown and Company, 1990), which has lists of seed companies that sell seeds for the hottest chiles. There are also quite a few companies on the Internet with hot chile seeds for sale.

Chiles develop their hottest flavor when they are fully ripe, so don't be tempted to pick them early. Plant them in full sun to really bring out the flavor. An important tip: wear rubber gloves when picking and preparing the hottest chiles. If the capsaicin gets on the skin of your hands, you don't want to accidentally touch your eyes or nose.

There are several ways to prepare your chiles for use as repellents. In dry powder form, chiles can be sprinkled around areas where rabbits and small creatures are nibbling. You can discourage deer from chewing on small tree trunks by dabbing on a paste made of pureed chiles. (Freeze the extra paste for later use.)

A tea made of chiles can be sprayed on plants and vegetables as a repellent, but care should be taken to check sensitive plants for burning first. Also, remember to wash the vegetables before eating them, unless you like them chile-flavored. If you like, you can add other ingredients, such as garlic, to your tea as well (see below).

Chile Tea

3 to 4 hot chiles, chopped (serranos and habaneros are
good choices)
1 quart boiling water

Add the chiles to the boiling water and let steep for 24 hours. Strain and discard the chiles. The solution should be quite strong, so on delicate plants you may want to dilute it by adding another quart of water. Play with this recipe until you find the perfect strength, always remembering to start weak and gradually move to a stronger solution. If the spray doesn't stick well to the plants, add a couple of drops of dishwashing liquid.

Eucalyptus

Eucalyptus has become more and more popular as a medicinal remedy, and now it's known to be an excellent insect repellent as well. The pungent odor of eucalyptus has much the same effect as cedar—and who hasn't heard of lining a closet with cedar to repel moths?

A NEW WORLD FRIEND

Eucalyptus trees are a fairly new arrival to many mild climates, but they've been grown in California since 1856. Early on, the trees were mostly used for windbreaks, shade, and firewood. Their popularity has since grown, and now they are a favorite landscape tree in many states.

When you crush eucalyptus leaves in your hands, the wonderful smell of the tree is released. Mulch made from eucalyptus and spread around your garden is sure to stop quite a few insects as well as animals.

If eucalyptus trees don't grow in your area, you can buy oil of eucalyptus at a health food store instead. The oil is a concentrated extract that can be diluted and sprayed on wood shavings for the same effect. The oil can also be used on a hummingbird feeder's hanger to deter ants from reaching the sugar solution.

Eucalyptus oil can be diluted to make a personal insect repellent. If you want to try it (and you don't mind smelling a bit like a eucalyptus tree), dilute the oil until there is just a faint odor of eucalyptus (try about $1/4$ teaspoon oil to 1 cup of water) and spray it on your skin. This repellent is said to work on fleas, ticks, chiggers, mosquitoes, and gnats as well. You may have to play with the amount of oil in the spray, adding more to keep those really pesky bugs away.

Now that you've made a spray that works for you, you can also spray it on your plants. One way to use this spray is on the borders of fences and lawns. Because eucalyptus oil is a good flea repellent, it may keep neighborhood fleas from entering your yard.

You can also make eucalyptus flea repellents for your pets. Dry eucalyptus leaves and crush them into a powder to use like flea powder, or make a spray like Eucalyptus Flea and Tick Repellent (see page 85).

Garlic

Garlic has long been known to have many beneficial qualities (besides warding off vampires) for both people and animals. It repels many of the major insect pests, especially aphids, and it has been shown to lessen the need for other control measures. Garlic is easy to grow, and mixed with your garden vegetables, it will afford them general insect protection.

GROWING GARLIC

Gardeners usually plant garlic in the spring, when they plant their gardens, but in warm and temperate climates, fall plantings are not uncommon. Garlic can be grown from seeds or cloves. It does best in full sun but will do nicely on a windowsill. Separate the garlic bulb into individual cloves and plant the cloves two inches deep and five inches apart in well draining soil or pots. It will sprout in ten to fourteen days and will require only water from then on to produce a bulb of good quality. Spring-planted garlic is usually ready to harvest in about 120 days; you can also leave it to reseed itself for the next year. Fall-planted garlic takes about nine months to harvest.

GARLIC AS A REPELLENT

- Garlic planted close to roses has been shown to protect the bushes from black spot, a fungus disease.
- As a companion crop, grown in rings around the crop to be protected, garlic has been particularly beneficial in repelling aphids from brussels sprouts, cabbage, and cauliflower.
- Feeding garlic to dogs is said to repel fleas. The recommended dose is one to two cloves a day, but adjust this amount depending on your dog's size. Parsley mixed with the garlic will help neutralize the garlic breath. (Parsley works for people, too!)
- A garlic tea (see below), sprayed on your plants, can provide protection from many insects, and even from animals, which dislike the garlic's odor. Garlic spray has also been credited with eliminating fungus and mildew on plants.

Garlic Tea

1 bulb of garlic, chopped
1 quart of hot water

Place the chopped garlic in the water and let steep for at least 24 hours. Strain and transfer to a spray bottle before use.

chapter eight

Four-Legged Intruders

CATS AND DOGS

Most of us, at one time or another, have been faced with the problem of unwanted animals in our yards and gardens. Whether they're dogs, cats, or other animals, they come to our yards to dig, forage for food, deposit feces, or just make a mess.

Sending that animal on its way

Use negative reinforcement to discourage animals from visiting your property. If a yard smells bad to an animal, it will often pass it by. Make your yard or garden as unattractive as possible by offending the animal's sense of smell. Our chile-garlic (page 142) and rotten egg (page 142) repellents are sure to have those animals turning up their noses at your plants.

Apply the chile-garlic mixture every few days for two to three weeks. The animals will hopefully find your property offensive for a long enough period of time that they'll get discouraged from using it. The rotten-smelling repellent should stay offensive to animals for about a week after applying, if the weather is dry.

Another way to keep dogs and cats or other animals out of desirable areas is to plant thorny bushes, such as pyracantha and barberry, around the edges of your yard. Where you don't want to plant hedges, just lay cuttings of the thorny bushes around the garden area to keep the animals out.

Hot and Garlicky Repellent

3 to 4 garlic cloves, crushed
3 to 4 hot chiles, chopped or pureed (habaneros work great)
1/2 teaspoon dishwashing liquid
3 gallons water

Mix all the ingredients together and let steep for 24 hours. Strain and dribble the mixture around your yard and garden.

Rotten-Smelling Repellent

6 eggs, beaten
6-ounce bottle of hot sauce (the hotter the better)
1 gallon water

Place all the ingredients in a large container with a tight-fitting lid. Shake until mixed and let sit for one week. Spray or dribble the foul-smelling mixture around your garden or yard.

DEER

Who hasn't marveled at one time or another at the gracefulness of deer? Unfortunately for gardeners, these gentle creatures can decimate a garden in no time flat. They will eat just about anything you plant and will come back time after time once they know food is available at your place.

Discouraging the dear deer

If you're tired of feeding your entire garden to deer every year, the best defense is a good offense—an offensive smell, that is. Deer use their sense of smell to detect predators and dangerous situations, so targeting this sense is one of the best and easiest ways to discourage them. Smells that seem odd to them trigger their defense mechanism, causing them to flee.

Plant Protect Sticks, which clip onto plants and emit a garlic smell, can be purchased at your local nursery. Strong-smelling soap bars can also be quite effective at controlling deer. Drill holes in the bars and hang them around the edges of your garden or from the limbs of trees. For best results, place the bars no more than three feet apart.

The smell of an animal's or person's hair will also deter deer. Place hair gathered from a pet groomer or hair stylist around the perimeter of prized plants, ringing the plant at its drip line so that the deer encounters the hair first, before the branches or stems of the plant. Placing the hair around the base of the plant will usually provide little help if the plant is large.

Urine of other animals is another effective deer repellent. If you don't have a dog to do the job for you, find a friendly dog-owning neighbor who will be happy to direct Fido to the right spots. Used cat litter sprinkled around the borders of your yard can also help send the deer away.

Many of the sprays and solutions used to deter other animals in this book will also work on deer. Any new smell that is unfamiliar to the deer will work. Baby powder, chile powder, or even clothes dryer sheets are worth a try when combating the destructive deer.

Keep in mind that deer are pretty clever animals; after a while, the new scent you are using to deter them will become familiar, and they will lose the desire to flee. You'll need to change or alternate the offensive smells in your yard to keep the deer wary. Keep track of which scents work and for how long, so you can use this information in planning your defense for the next year. However, in very severe conditions, like during droughts and floods, hungry deer will eat anything green no matter what it smells like.

Another fact that should be noted: if your yard is especially tempting, with many of your local deer's favorite foods, offensive smells may not be enough of a deterrent.

You can also try making your plants taste bad by spraying them with a bitter solution. Make your own bitter sprays with horseradish, hot chiles, or vinegar mixed with water, or try using a commercial bitter apple spray. (Your homemade solution should be strong enough to be pretty bitter to your taste buds.) Unfortunately, these sprays work only when the deer starts eating your plants, so some damage will occur using this method. Don't forget to wash the bitter solutions off plants you plan to eat, or you will have the same reaction as the deer.

Finally, if all else fails (and sometimes it does), fencing and barriers may be the only ways to keep your garden free of deer. Because deer are fairly large, a good fence should be at least eight feet high. Wire mesh placed around and over plants will also be quite effective. Electric fence wires are also available in extreme cases.

Deer-resistant plants

There are some plants that deer don't particularly like (although, again, a hungry deer may eat just about anything). The following is a partial list of common plants and trees not favored by our four-legged friends. Check with your local nursery for a complete list of plants available in your area.

Alyssum	Baby's Breath	Brunnera
American Elder	Bamboo	Buttercup
American Holly	Barberry	Butterfly Bush and
American Wisteria	Basil	Weed
Anise	Bee Balm	Cactus
Artemisia	Begonia	California Fuchsia
Asiatic Jasmine	Bleeding Heart	California Poppy
Asparagus	Bluebell	Calla Lily
Australian Pine	Bluebonnet	Cape Honeysuckle
Autumn Sage	Broom	Carnation

Carolina Jessamine

Catnip

Clematis

Colorado Blue Spruce

Common Lilac

Coneflower

Corydalis

Cosmos

Daffodil

Desert Willow

Douglas Fir

Dusty Miller

Eastern Red Cedar

Eastern White Pine

European Privet

Fig

Flowering Dogwood

Geranium

Gerbera Daisy

Ginkgo

Gladiolus

Hakonechloa

Heliotrope

Hellebore

Iris

Jacob's Ladder

Jasmine

Juniper

Kenilworth Ivy

Lamb's Ears

Lavender

Lily of the Nile

Lithodora

Lobelia

Lupine

Mahonia

Marigold

Marjoram

Mimosa

Mint

Mock Orange

Morning Glory

Mountain Laurel

Nandina

Oleander

Oregano

Oriental Poppy

Peony

Phlomis

Potentilla

Rhododendron

Rhubarb

Periwinkle

Pieris

Pulmonaria

Rose of Sharon

Sage

Sarcococca (Sweet Box)

Shasta Daisy

Snapdragon

Snowberry

Society Garlic

Spice Bush

Saint-John's-Wort

Statice

Sugar Maple

Sumac

Sunflower

Sweet Pea

Sweet William

Tansy

Texas Buckeye

Thyme

Trumpetvine

Tulip Tree

Verbena

Veronica

Vinca

Violets

Viburnum

Wax Begonia

Wild Ginger

Winter Jasmine

Yarrow

Yucca

Zinnia

The life of a deer

Deer are members of the mammal family Cervidae, which also includes moose, elk, and caribou. Most deer species average around 400 pounds. The moose is the largest of the deer species, weighing up to 1,200 pounds.

All deer leave a split-hoof imprint that looks like two toes. The males have antlers that they shed every year; in some species, the females also have antlers. Deer, which are cud-chewing herbivores, lack top front teeth—and you have to wonder how they eat without them. They can eat great quantities of food and can completely strip trees and shrubs in times of famine.

Female deer become sexually mature at about age one and a half and males at about age two and a half. In late summer, the rutting (breeding) season begins for most species. After breeding, females usually give birth to a fawn in late spring. Normally, just one fawn is born, but twins are not uncommon.

GOPHERS

Fan-shaped mounds of dirt are appearing in your yard and garden. You've even noticed whole plants missing. Sounds like you may be a victim of the dreaded gopher.

Going after the gopher

People have tried many methods to rid their yards of gophers. Some are more successful than others, depending on the conditions of one's yard. One secret is to start treatment immediately upon seeing the first signs of gophers, before the tunneling is extensive and much harder to treat. Gophers are opportunistic and will take over an abandoned burrow if they can. Often just one remedy is not enough to deter gophers, so try various combinations of the following deterrents to find the right solution for you.

- Plant gopher plants (*Euphorbia lathyrus*; available at your local nursery) two to three feet apart around your prized garden. Many gardeners swear that gophers dislike this plant and will avoid it. (See page 136.)

- Other plants also known to deter gophers are daffodils and castor bean plants. **Warning:** Castor bean plants are extremely poisonous and probably should not be planted where pets or children can get near them.

- Placing newspapers around your plants and yard is an old trick that may keep a gopher from surfacing. However, it doesn't keep a gopher from tunneling under your plants and eating the roots!

- Dumping used kitty litter, dog droppings, or hair clippings into the gopher's tunnel may convince it there's a predator nearby and encourage it to leave. This is a good method to try in a small yard or garden. You might have to repeat this method a few times to prove to the gopher that a predator is around.

- Scaring gophers away is a popular method; many people swear by whirligigs or pinwheels placed around their yards. It is believed the vibrations that these devices transmit into the ground annoy or scare the gophers and force them to find a new home elsewhere. Some ultrasonic devices now sold for this very purpose claim to protect an area from rodents (including gophers) for up to one thousand square yards.

- Sound deterrents, which work along the same lines as whirligigs, may also help. Try leaving empty soda bottles around your yard, anchored or partially buried for best results. The noise produced when the wind passes over the bottles will scare away many forms of wildlife.

- A good way to protect your garden from gophers is to line your garden beds both on the sides and the bottom with chicken wire. This requires a lot of work to sink the wire "basket" at least eighteen to twenty-four inches deep. Be sure to connect the sides and bottom of the basket securely to eliminate any holes that the gopher could find. This method works best for raised-bed gardens. Gopher wire is another helpful solution.

- While the gopher is above ground, it is an easy target for many predators, including cats, owls, and foxes. However, few predators, except for snakes and some members of the weasel family, will tackle the territorial gopher down in its burrow. Although most people don't want weasels or snakes in their yards either, a large king snake is a predator that most gardeners should be happy to have around. They not only will eat any rodent, but also will eat rattlesnakes.

- Packing dry ice in the tunnel in high concentrations will suffocate the gopher. This method works best when the tunnels aren't very extensive. At the very least, it will send the gopher elsewhere for the moment.

- The old method of placing a hose down the gopher's hole to flush it out is still effective, especially if the gopher's tunneling system is small. Do this in the morning and evening when the gopher is most active. Use barbecue tongs to catch the gopher if it emerges from the flooded hole. Drop the gopher in a bucket and dispatch as you please.

- The old-fashioned gopher trap, like the Macabee trap that is available at garden and home centers, is still popular with many people. If you love this trap, make it more effective with the right use of the equipment and the right bait. First, to locate the burrow you will need to make or buy a gopher probe. The probe can be a stick or dowel if you have soft soils, but for hard or dry soils a probe with an enlarged tip that is wider than the shaft of the probe (like a narrow shovel or trowel) will make locating the tunnels easier. Trapping in the main burrow is more effective than the lateral burrows. To find the main burrow, probe about eight to twelve inches from the plug side of the mound (the side with the hole). When the probe penetrates the burrow, the probe will drop quickly about two inches or so. This is where you want to put the trap. Now for the right bait. Place a sprig of flowering star jasmine or tomato leaves over the tripping mechanism or behind the trap. These baits have a strong scent that attracts the gopher. Gardeners with serious gopher problems should keep a pot of jasmine handy. Another good bait is whatever plant is under attack by the gopher. If they like it that much, use it to catch them. And some gardeners swear by a bait of raisins placed behind the trap.

- Gopher poisons and baits are popular choices in the fight against gophers because of their ease of use and there are no traps to empty. Just remember that these are poisons, and try to use them only as a last resort when other methods fail. Always use the recommended applicator and store these products away from children and pets. And bear in mind that any wildlife that ingests the poisoned gopher will also be poisoned if the poison used does not state there is no secondary kill.

The lonely life of a gopher

There are thirty-three different species of gophers, but the species with which most people are familiar, and with which they have the most difficulty, is the pocket gopher. Pocket gophers were named for the fur-lined pouches or pockets inside their cheeks, which they use to carry food. Like all gophers, pocket gophers are rodents. They are varying shades of brown, five to nine inches long, with short legs and long curved claws designed for digging.

Most of the time gophers are loners; they are very protective of their tunnels and will defend them against invaders. One gopher can have an elaborate tunnel system that can cover about seven hundred square yards of ground. The tunneling can be deep or shallow, and generally there is one main tunnel with many side tunnels. Gophers, being great soil cultivators and aerators, prefer soft soils with good drainage, but they can also be found in gardens with different soil quality.

Gophers do not hibernate (unlike ground squirrels, which do), and they can feed day and night all year round. As they tunnel, they will feed on any delicious roots they find.

Gophers generally give birth to a litter of four offspring in the spring. Sometimes, in warm climates, gopher females will have two litters in a season. The babies are usually pushed out of the mother's burrow after six weeks to find their own territory.

MOLES

Oh, no—you've found signs of tunneling just under the surface in your garden or yard. You might have even found some dirt pushed to the surface but no exit hole. Gophers again? Actually, it sounds like you probably have a mole.

Mole holes

First, you need to determine which tunnels are active and which ones are just for foraging. Step on and press down all the tunnels (sometimes they look like ridges) in your yard. The mole will repair the main tunnels. Moles can dig about two hundred feet per day if necessary, in search of worms and insects.

There are several strategies that may help you rid yourself of this subterranean dweller. Because moles are very sensitive to ground vibrations, the whirligigs and vibration-producing products mentioned on page 147 may help deter them. Placing dog or cat droppings in the tunnels may convince a mole that a predator is nearby, causing it to leave. Also, moles dislike very wet soils, so soaking their tunnels may also deter them.

Moles are known to dislike castor bean plants, which are very poisonous and should be planted only with extreme caution. However, a spray made out of castor oil may also discourage a mole. Cats have taken their toll on moles, and moles definitely try to avoid these predators. However, cats will often carry home a mole and refuse to eat it. It is thought the mole's musty odor makes it an unappetizing catch.

Trapping is sometimes the best method to control moles. Various traps are made for this purpose. Two very effective traps are the spear traps for new surface tunnels and the deep tunnel traps. Early spring and fall are generally the best times to catch moles, though you can try at any time. When the weather is very cold or hot the moles move deeper into their tunnels and you may not know they are there. There is no baiting of mole traps because you are using the mole's biology against itself. The trap blocks the tunnel and works because the mole wants to reopen his tunnels and by doing so triggers the trap. Follow traps directions, but some trial and error may be necessary to get rid of the moles.

Insect eaters

Unlike gophers, moles are not rodents. They belong to the mammal order Insectivora, which gives you a clue to their habits. Moles eat insects, grubs, and worms, but not plants. Moles won't eat your garden plants, but their tunneling activities in search of insects and worms can certainly create unplanned changes in your yard. Many people who are trying to garden in harmony with nature feel a mole's beneficial role as a natural soil aerator outweighs any damage they do.

Moles range in size from $2^{1}/_{2}$ to 6 inches in length, with short tails. Their fur is usually brown to black and they have very broad front feet, which they use to swim through the soil. Their eyes are very small (about the size of a pinhead), and they have no external ears. Moles generally have one litter of four young per year, usually in the spring. The young are independent in about a month.

Moles are very territorial and are active both day and night. They are in constant search of food and prefer living in soft soils. You usually will not see a mole in extremely dry or wet soil, or where there are a lot of rocks. Because of their need to consume large quantities of insects, it is estimated that only two or three moles can survive per acre.

Mole Repellent

> 2 tablespoons castor oil
> 1 tablespoon dishwashing liquid
> 1 gallon water
>
> Mix all ingredients together, and wet down the mole's tunnels with the solution.

OPOSSUMS

Opossums, those large and unique-looking creatures, have decided your yard is a diner's delight and are proceeding to eat everything (and we do mean everything) in sight. No matter how many times you scare them away, they keep coming back. Can they really be that smart?

Smarter than they look

Opossums are good climbers and can scale most fences. Barriers, electric wires on tops of fences, and metal strips on fences (which keep the opossum from getting a grip) can help deter them. Despite their slow movement and poor vision, which makes them appear dim-witted, opossums are fairly intelligent and will usually find a way around or under the barriers. They can be pretty persistent at times.

Opossums are scavengers looking for anything to eat. The more accessible the food, the better. Opossums have been seen eating road kills, pet food left out overnight, mice, and just about any garden plant. Their front paws are very human-like, and when they pick up something to eat, they look like Bugs Bunny eating a carrot. Opossums are very fond of fruit, so ripe fruit, especially grapes, makes excellent bait.

Trash cans are a favorite target, as are compost piles. The smell of ripe trash can drive an opossum into a feeding frenzy! You can use this knowledge to trap an unwanted opossum. Place an empty trash can next to a fence or porch where the opossum can easily jump down on it. Next place the trash can lid on top of the trash can, upside down and tilted so it will turn if pushed. Put a favorite opossum food, like grapes or bacon, on the tilted lid on the low side. When the opossum jumps onto the lid for the food, the lid will turn over quickly, dropping the opossum into the trash can. Now he can be relocated to the back country, far away from your garden. Remember to check local laws before relocating the opossum.

Commercial Havahart live traps also work quite well for capturing opossums. You can usually rent these from your local animal shelter or feed store. Remember to wear gloves when transporting any wild animal. Even with the opossum's easygoing nature and its habit of playing dead when truly frightened, it will bite if it feels threatened. Opossums have fifty teeth, more than any other mammal, and they are all sharp.

Playing dead—a way of life

Opossums are commonly called possums, but true possums are a different animal that lives in Australia. The common opossum (*Didelphis virginiana*) is the only North American marsupial. Their bodies average fifteen to twenty inches in length, with an additional nine to twenty inches for their prehensile tail, and they can weigh between nine and thirteen pounds. Opossums are nocturnal and usually find a nice place under a deck or porch to sleep during the day. Opossums can have up to fourteen young in a litter, but ten offspring per litter is more common. Females usually have two litters per year. The young are born after only thirteen days of gestation and stay with the female for about two months. The average life span of an opossum is seven years, so you may find the same opossum back in your yard, year after year after year.

In many large cities, opossums are becoming so common that they are considered pests, and animal shelters are being asked to take part in controlling the opossum population. Because many cities do not have the funds to do such a job, homeowners have often had to find ways to deal with the persistent opossum on their own.

Q: Why did the chicken cross the road?

A: To prove to the opossum that it can be done.

The point of this riddle is that opossums are slow *and* have poor eyesight—a deadly combination when crossing busy streets. Despite this disadvantage, opossums are one of a handful of species that are flourishing near humankind.

RABBITS

Your garden looked great when you retired for the evening, but by the time you awakened, rows off seedling vegetables had been chewed to the ground. Small holes dug under your fence and telltale footprints point to a bunny attack. Those cute little rabbits can practically eat their weight in your garden produce in one night!

Keeping those bunnies away

Cages placed around young seedlings have long been used to deter hungry rabbits, and they are still an excellent method of exclusion. Old milk and yogurt cartons, strawberry baskets, and wire all make good cages. Light cages like strawberry baskets may need a stone on top to weigh it down. In areas of heavy rabbit infestation, the cages may need to be stronger and completely cover desired crops. Check the cages to be sure they are securely anchored so the bunnies don't go under the cage and defeat your effort.

Use the rabbit's keen nose against him and convince him a predator is near by placing dog hair or dog droppings around the plants in your garden or along the fence. You can also make a rabbit repellent spray (see page 155).

A product called Plant Protect Sticks, available at nurseries, claims to repel bunnies (and deer too) with a garlic odor. The sticks resemble small writing pens that clip onto the ends of plants. When the seal is broken, the stick emits the offensive scent. Another scent-based repellent, DeFence, comes from the makers of the Havahart live trap and uses a rotten egg smell to repel rabbits. This product also has a stronger version that mixes eggs with garlic and capsaicin; when dried, it is odorless to humans. You can make a similar solution by mixing eggs, crushed garlic, and chile powder and leaving it out to rot for several days. Then spray or dribble it around your yard. Havahart also sells a motion detector that shoots a three-second spray of water. Between the water spray and the sprinkler sound, this may send the rabbit on its way.

Another antirabbit tactic using scent is to sprinkle blood meal (available at places that sell organic fertilizer) around your yard. The smell of blood will repel the bunnies. In addition to ridding your yard of rabbits, blood meal is a great plant fertilizer and can be sprinkled around most plants. However, be sure to water thoroughly after applying the blood meal or it could burn your lawn or plants.

Landscaping with plants that rabbits don't particularly like can help; just realize that a very hungry rabbit isn't deterred by much. Gardeners can reduce damage by planting allium, irises, anise hyssop, baptisia, bee balm, catmint, fritillaria, hellebore, lavender, peony, salvia, oriental poppies, veronica, yarrow, daffodils, daylilies, lamb's ears, and sedum to deter rabbits. Rabbits may avoid a shady garden that is planted with hostas, foxgloves, and astilbes.

Several common treatments for repelling rabbits require making the plants they're after taste bad. Sprinkling the plants with red pepper powder, sulfur, or lime is said to leave a bitter taste in a rabbit's mouth. Check your plants for burning, especially if you use the sulfur. If you are treating vegetables, wash well before eating. Here are two easily made vegetable washes:

- 1 teaspoon Lysol in 1 gallon water
- 3 ounces Epsom salts in 1 gallon water

Trapping rabbits is fairly easy with a Havahart live trap. Place the trap in your garden along a walkway or, if you know how the rabbits are getting in, by the entrance hole to your yard. Bait with their favorite garden plant, alfalfa, or fruit.

Rabbit Repellent

4 cloves garlic
2 cups hot water
1 teaspoon fish emulsion

Steep the garlic in the hot water. When cool, discard the garlic and add the fish emulsion. To use, dilute 1 tablespoon of this concentrate in 1 cup of water and spray around your garden plants.

The life of Peter Cottontail

Rabbits are timid creatures that are generally gray or brown in color. They usually come out in the late evening and early morning to forage for food, but some of the fifteen common American species of rabbits and hares are active during the day. They prefer young plants or the tender ends of bushes and shrubs.

Rabbits are not rodents, as many people believe, but belong to the order Lagomorpha. Like rodents, rabbits have two large front incisor teeth, but, unlike rodents, rabbits also have a smaller pair of incisors, called peg teeth, directly behind the front two.

The sheer number of rabbits is the biggest problem for most gardeners. Rabbits do indeed breed prolifically, with rabbit litters averaging four to eight young. A female rabbit can easily have six litters a year. The high breeding rate is necessary because rabbits are a major prey species, and it is estimated that only about 1 percent of wild rabbits survive for three years.

SKUNKS

Skunks are digging up your lawn and raiding your yard. No way are you going outside to chase them away. Yelling at the varmints from your upstairs window hasn't scared them off either. What can you do?

Solving a smelly problem

First, try keeping the skunks out of your yard. Plug any holes in or under your fence with rocks or rose cuttings to block their access. Skunks usually use the same paths in and out of your yard. Around an unfenced yard, either place a two-foot-high wire fence or lay very loose chicken wire directly on the ground. Skunks do not like to walk on unsteady ground (cats feel the same way, so this is a good way to, for example, keep cats from using your freshly sown vegetable beds as a litter box). In spring, female skunks will be looking for places to dig a den to have their babies. Skunks will make their dens under porches and decks or dig a dirt den under shrubs or hollow trees. Block any such areas early in the season, or you could have a family of skunks move in.

If blocking or fencing the skunk out is not possible, then a water assault could help. There are sprinklers on the market with built-in motion sensors. Set them where the skunk usually enters your yard. One downside to these sprinklers is that they are often expensive. A good alternative is a blast from a child's water gun. Use the big "Super Soaker" that can send a blast of water hundreds of feet for this purpose. Keep the soaker ready and give the skunk a quick blast of water—but be careful, as a water blast face-to-face is a sure way to get a skunk mad at you. So make sure it is a sneak attack and the skunk cannot see you.

Get rid of all food sources in your yard. Never leave your pet's food dish out overnight. This is like ringing a dinner bell to skunks, raccoons, and many other animals. If the skunk digs to look for grubs, try spraying beneficial nematodes on problem areas to kill the grubs. These nematodes (see page 126) are minute parasitic worms that attack only specific organisms, like grubs. An additional benefit is they also kill other soil pests, like fleas and cutworms. Beneficial nematodes can be purchased at most nurseries or by mail order. Follow the directions carefully when applying. Nematodes need a moist environment to survive and do not like direct sunlight, so it's best to apply them in the late evening after the soil or lawn has been moistened.

Skunks are pretty easy to trap with a live trap baited with cooked bacon. Removing the skunk is another problem, but many animal control agencies will remove the skunk for you.

If your local animal control won't help, some local wildlife organizations might. Check with them first. The worse possible scenario is that you will have to remove the skunk yourself. Skunks can carry rabies, so be very careful. Wear gloves and goggles (a skunk's spray can cause temporary blindness). Cut a small slit the size of the trap's handle in a thick tarp. If you are using a Havahart-style trap with a handle on top, cut the slit in the middle of the tarp. Holding the tarp in front of you, so you can see through the slit and the skunk can't see you, walk up to the trapped skunk, slowly placing the tarp down over the trap, and aligning the slit with the handle. Let the frightened skunk lie in the dark under the tarp for a few minutes until it calms down. Wrap the tarp around the trap and transport the captured creature off your property to a remote location. For a safety measure, place the tarp-covered trap in a plastic garbage can with the lid on to keep the skunk's smell out of your car! When releasing the skunk, keep the trap covered when opening the trap door and then step back out of the spray zone (though at this point most skunks just want to get to a safe place and away from the trap).

Finally, many of you who own dogs know they usually do a good job at keeping skunks out of your yard, but there are few pet experiences worse than a dog that has just been sprayed by a startled skunk. The next time this happens, instead of reaching for the tomato juice, try the easy recipe on page 158 that really works. It cuts through the greasy skunk spray to wash it off and gets rid of the odor, too.

The life of a skunk

Skunks belong to the family Mustelidae, along with weasels, ferrets, and minks. All have a scent gland, of which the skunk's is the strongest-smelling one. Long ago in Europe, scent glands from animals in this family were used to make a base for perfume.

Four species of skunks are native to North America, with the striped skunk being the most common. They are about two feet long, not including the tail, and can weigh up to fourteen pounds (that's one big skunk). Its cousin, the spotted skunk, is much smaller. When threatened, most skunks will stand on their front feet and spray directly over their heads.

Skunks are usually nocturnal and their odor tells everyone that a skunk has been prowling around. Their diet consists mainly of insects and small rodents, and in this regard, skunks are very beneficial. When skunks dig up a lawn or garden, they are usually looking for grubs and other insect goodies, but at times they will eat roots and plants.

Skunks will dig a den in the ground or find a nice spot under a house or patio in which to sleep and have their young. Generally, skunks have only one litter of young a year, with the litter averaging five young. The skunk mother keeps the babies with her for the first year.

Best Skunk Smell Remover Solution

1 cup 3-percent hydrogen peroxide
$1/4$ cup baking soda
Grease-cutting dishwashing liquid detergent

Combine the peroxide and baking soda in a container. Slowly add the detergent until the mixture is the consistency of gravy. Wash your pet with the mixture. Do not get the mixture into the pet's eyes (or your eyes). Use any leftover mixture to wash areas or towels with the odor on them, but do not store the remainder. Baking soda and peroxide form a gas that can break a tightly sealed container.

GROUND SQUIRRELS

Holes without mounds of dirt around them have started appearing in your yard. Nearly every plant has been nibbled on, and some—especially fruits, seeds, and berries—have been eaten completely. Yes, the cute little brown squirrels you see scurrying about are eating their way through your garden and yard.

Squirrel, squirrel, go away

Like gophers, ground squirrels are very difficult to control once they have decided your yard is the perfect habitat. The trial-and-error method is the best approach for controlling them. If one remedy doesn't work, try another, or even mix remedies to find the perfect combination for your yard. The following are a few methods that have worked under a variety of conditions.

Try trapping them using a Havahart live trap baited with nuts, fruit, or peanut butter. This can be an ongoing battle, but it works! Janet caught twenty-seven squirrels over the course of several weeks by baiting the trap with walnuts. Check to see whether your local animal control will pick up the animals for you and what the laws are concerning relocating the squirrels if you catch one. Always wear gloves when setting and retrieving the trap, and *never* handle a ground squirrel. Some ground squirrels are known to carry the fleas that can transmit Rocky Mountain spotted fever. Fortunately, no cases of the fever have been reported in recent years.

Squirrels are known to dislike plants sprayed with a chile pepper solution, so try making your own chile spray to deter them. Keep in mind that you may have to play with the amount of chiles (some are stronger than others) to get the perfect concentration to do the job.

Rototilling or turning over the soil regularly will destroy the squirrel's burrows. An extra deterrent is to rototill dog or cat droppings into the burrows. If the burrows are too deep or in a place where you can't turn the soil over, then pack the burrow holes with the droppings. The squirrels will think a predator is nearby and ideally will find a new home elsewhere.

Grapes and other hanging fruit are a perfect treat for squirrels. Try tying brown paper bags over low-hanging fruit to deter them. (This trick also keeps birds from eating your fruit.)

Squirrels love freshly planted seeds, so try placing chicken wire over beds to discourage squirrels from digging. Anchor the wire down, or the squirrels will just go under it.

Flat metal bands about twelve inches wide, flared at the bottom if necessary, will help prevent squirrels from climbing into trees. Be sure to place the bands high enough up the tree trunks so the squirrels can't jump over them.

Ground squirrels are a favorite prey of snakes. If you find a king snake or gopher snake in your yard, just send it down one of the holes! Seriously, these snakes are just the predators to solve your problem, although you'll have to hope they will find the hole on their own. The squirrels will leave immediately! (With any luck, never to return.)

If there is a tall tree branch is near or over the ground squirrel holes, remove the leaves from it to make the perfect perch for hawks, which love ground squirrel for lunch.

One wild remedy suggests depositing male human urine in the squirrel's hole to send those squirrels packing.

If you don't mind the thought of killing the ground squirrels, the "Rat Zapper" has been shown to be pretty effective. Though the product is not marketed for squirrels, there have been reports of good success with this product.

Destructive diggers

Ground squirrels, which are a major pest problem, belong to the rodent family Sciuridae, which also includes tree squirrels and chipmunks. These digging rodents have cost taxpayers millions of dollars in damage to roadways, airport runways, and flood control levees. They weaken structures by undermining them, forcing replacement. The eradication measures necessary to get rid of the squirrels themselves drive the costs up even more. This damage is on top of the damage squirrels do to crops and gardens.

Ground squirrels are fairly large rodents, ranging in size from nine to eleven inches, not including the tail, which can be another five to nine inches long. They can weigh from one pound to a little over two pounds. Unlike most squirrels, ground squirrels live in colonies. They usually have two litters each year, averaging seven young per litter. The babies are born in the spring and summer months and usually stay with the parents for about ten weeks. Squirrels and chipmunks usually hibernate, but in very warm regions they may skip the hibernation and feed all year round.

The burrows of ground squirrels are sometimes very elaborate, with secret entrances. Most squirrels are active during the day, foraging for food or working on their burrows. The squirrels dig out specific chambers in their burrows, using some for storage and others for nesting. Usually there will be a network of paths between the entrance holes on the surface, so the squirrel is never far from a hole. In the winter, if it is cold enough for the squirrels to hibernate, they close up the entrance holes with plant material.

Squirrel Chile Spray

4 hot chiles (habanero, serrano, jalapeño, or similar)
3 gallons water
1 teaspoon dishwashing liquid

Puree the chiles with 2 to 3 cups of the water. Strain the puree and discard the solids (the bits of chile would clog a sprayer). Add the rest of the water to the chile solution. Add the dishwashing liquid. Spray around plants, but check for burning before spraying directly on them.

TREE SQUIRRELS

Tree squirrels are cute and fun to watch, but they soon lose their appeal when they are eating your vegetable garden or raiding your bird feeder. You have tried everything to discourage them from helping themselves to your plants or feeder. Is there anything you can do to stop them?

Can you beat the squirrels?

Prevailing over these critters depends on how badly you want to win the battle. These small rodents are quite resourceful and clever. If they want something badly enough, they will work hard to get it.

Many commercial squirrel deterrents are made with cayenne pepper, and it is said the squirrels are very sensitive to this irritant. It can be purchased at just about any grocery store, and usually a little goes a long way. The main active ingredient in cayenne pepper is capsaicin; we talked a lot about it in our section on chiles (see page 137). Capsaicin is in many chiles, so a spray made with the hottest chiles should really help repel the squirrels. Try our chile repellent on page 161. Experiment with it and see what works for your situation. Remember, you will need to reapply any repellent after it rains. Also, if you are applying a chile repellent to vegetables, remember to wash them well before you eat them.

Keep in mind that just repelling squirrels usually doesn't work long term, especially if you have a large area to protect. Many factors play into any control program. The native food availability is very important. When abundant food is available there is less pressure on squirrels to raid your garden. Conversely, during bad weather the squirrels may not be able to forage, making your yard very attractive. A large squirrel population can deplete the native food supply quickly and drive squirrels to forage for other food. Of course, if you are planting their favorite foods and they are easy to get to, your garden has just become the local Squirrel-Mart grocery store. You need a good squirrel control program to keep the squirrels out.

We've talked about repellents, but how about exclusion? A physical barrier—like row covers, fencing, and trimming back tree branches that provide access to your garden—will help to keep them out of your vegetables. Try wrapping small sapling trees with netting or plastic to protect them. When you are trying to protect larger trees, the process becomes more difficult. You'll need to wrap the trunk with sheet metal or a flexible piece of plastic. The barrier must be wide enough, at least two feet or wider, to prevent the squirrel from jumping over it. Fasten the barrier in a way that allows you to expand it as the tree grows.

Relocating the squirrels is also an option *if* that is allowed by state or local regulations. Check before trapping. It is always a good idea to not trap during breeding season or you might create orphaned squirrel kittens. Live trapping is pretty easy if you use some of the squirrels' favorite foods—things like breakfast cereal, nuts, sunflower seeds, grains, apples, or popcorn.

Bird feeders

Squirrels just can't ignore the lure of a well-stocked bird feeder. There are lots of ideas for making your feeders squirrel-proof. There are baffles, cones, and other contraptions to prevent the squirrel from reaching your feeder. Then there are commercial products that make the seed taste bad to the squirrels (without bothering the birds). Bird lovers have tried, with various degrees of success, to suspend their bird feeders on a thin rope or wire so the squirrels can't reach it. Then we can watch the squirrels do an entertaining high-wire act. I have even heard of people rigging a low-voltage wire to the pole of a bird feeder to keep the squirrels away. My favorite is giving the squirrel its own feeder, but admittedly that only breeds more squirrels.

Ground squirrel relative

There are over a hundred different species of tree squirrel worldwide, and they can be found on every continent except Antarctica. The real difference between ground squirrels and tree squirrels is their habitat. Flying squirrels are quite different, however, with their modified skin flaps for gliding.

The male and female tree squirrels look alike, and their tails are about the same length as their bodies. The female mates twice a year, giving birth to between four and eight kittens in a nest called a *dray*. Tree squirrels live about five to seven years. They communicate with barks, chatters, screams, and purrs—some people say they sound like noisy birds. Squirrels also communicate by stamping their feet, moving their tails, and walking in a certain way.

Squirrels are mostly vegetarians—their favorite foods are nuts, berries, seeds, and tree buds—but they will eat some insects, small birds, and bird eggs. Squirrels collect nuts and bury them in the soil as a provision for winter. Interestingly, squirrels can remember where they have hidden the nuts because their memory increases by 15 percent in the fall.

Common species of tree squirrels in the United States are the North American fox squirrel and the Eastern gray squirrel. Squirrels are considered game animals, and many people enjoy hunting and eating them. The American Heart Association has found that squirrel meat is low in fat but high in cholesterol.

Squirrels are active during the daytime hours and in many cities they have become the most common type of rodent that people see. Squirrels have adapted to live quite close to humans and are very good at begging in parks or raiding gardens. Because squirrels are rodents, they must chew to sharpen their continuously growing teeth. Unfortunately, they will occasionally chew on trees and even on power lines, causing power outages.

VOLES

It seems you are being invaded by gophers or ground squirrels because you're finding lots of open holes in the ground and your plants are under attack. Something is chewing the bark of trees, eating the roots of lawns and devouring garden plants. Then you notice what looks like mice running around during the day along runs between these holes. Do you have a multispecies invasion? No, you probably have voles.

Sending the vole packing

Most of the deterrents for mice and rats (see page 25) will work for voles. But because voles tend to be active in the daylight hours, you can also set up some predator pest control.

If your yard or property is large, one of the best things you can do is put up a hawk pole. If you've ever visited San Diego's Safari Park, you've probably seen poles about fifteen to twenty feet tall, with perches on top. These poles encourage hawks and owls to come to the area and prey on the rodent population. If you don't want to erect a new pole in your yard but you do have a large tree, you can remove some of the leaves from one branch to make a good landing area for hawks and owls.

To discourage the voles, make their habitat less appealing to them by removing weeds, heavy mulch, and dense ground covers that provide food and protection from predators. We want the natural predators to keep their numbers down. Regular mowing of weeds near your home or garden will reduce vole invasion. By mowing a clear area (fifteen feet is ideal), the voles will have no protection and be less likely to cross it. When vole numbers are high, a four-foot-wide area around young trees should also be kept free of plants and mulch. This deters the voles a little more because they do not like to feed in the open.

Sometimes fencing is a good option; a tightly woven wire fence (mesh $1/4$ inch or smaller) at least twelve inches high will help keep the voles out. Be sure to bury the bottom of the fencing six to ten inches below ground to prevent the voles from digging under the fence. For extra effectiveness, keep the area around the fence free of vegetation.

Trapping may be necessary, and simple mouse traps will work quite well. Always set the traps on the vole's runs. This is critical, because voles seldom stray from their runways. You can bait the traps with peanut butter or apples but usually that is not necessary. It is best to set the traps at a right angle in the runway. Because voles can carry infectious diseases, always use rubber or disposable gloves when handling traps and dead voles.

A mouse's cousin

Voles are rodents that can be found throughout North America. They resemble mice, but they're usually brownish-gray, with long fur and short ears. The biggest difference is that voles have tails *shorter* than the length of their bodies. Vole adults average about five inches in length and can produce four to five litters of five young each per year. One meadow vole in captivity had seventeen litters in one year! That's eighty-five new pests in a year from just one mother.

Resources and Buying Guide

Throughout this book, we've often referred to commercially available beneficial insects. In this section, we provide a short list of some of the commonly requested beneficial organisms. Many more beneficial organisms are available for purchase, and complete lists can be obtained from suppliers, a number of whom are listed in this section.

Some of the beneficial organisms that are mentioned in this book occur only in nature and are not available for sale. For more information concerning the beneficial insects or organisms that would be appropriate and available for your use, contact your local nursery or agricultural extension or one of the many beneficial-insect suppliers who do consulting for the public.

Remember that there may be government restrictions on or permits required for the shipment and release of certain biological control organisms in your state. The supplier should know the regulations, but before purchasing any organism, make sure you know the regulations or restrictions by consulting your local or state agriculture department.

COMMONLY PURCHASED PREDATORS AND THEIR PREY

Chrysoperla and *Chrysopa* spp.: green lacewings, a predator of aphids.

Coccinella septempunctata: seven-spotted ladybird beetle, a predator of aphids.

Cotesia melanoscelus: a parasite of gypsy moth larvae.

Cryptolaemus montrouzieri: mealybug destroyer, predator of mealybugs and scales.

Delphastus pusillus: small ladybird beetle, a predator of whiteflies.

Deraeocoris brevis: a true bug, a predator of *Lygus* bugs, whiteflies, pear psylla, aphids, thrips, and loopers.

Encarsia formosa: a parasitic wasp, predator of greenhouse whitefly.

Galendromus occidentalis: a predatory mite, predator of western spider mite.

Gambusia affinis: mosquito fish, a predator of mosquitoes.

Heterorhabditis bacteriophora: a parasitic nematode, predator of mature flies, caterpillars, weevil larvae, and other soil-dwelling insects.

Hippodamia convergens: a convergent ladybird beetle, a predator of aphids and for general control.

Orius spp.: minute pirate bugs, predators of aphids.

Podisus maculiventris: spined soldier bug, a predator of gypsy moths and other insects.

Rhyzobius lophanthae: black-brown ladybird beetle, a predator of various scales.

Steinnernema carpocapsae: a parasitic nematode, predator of caterpillars, beetle larvae, and other soil-dwelling insects.

Tenodera aridifolia sinensis: praying mantis, predator for general control.

Trichogramma spp.: parasitic wasps, predators of exposed eggs of various moths and butterflies.

Typholdromus pyri: a predatory mite, predator of apple and other orchard mites.

INTERNET RESOURCES

There are lots of sites now with great information on organic gardening, pest control, and where to purchase beneficial insects. Many of these sites have newsletters, blogs, and ideas for the home gardener. Below we have named just a few that have been particularly helpful to us and others. Keep in mind that the Internet is ever-changing; use your favorite search engine to seek out new resources.

- One of our favorite sites is www.whatsthatbug.com. It is a great site for identifying insects. Take a digital picture and upload to the site, and they will tell you what it is. The site also has a great picture gallery.

- Another fun site is the Pest Wizard at www.pestwizard.com. We really like the section "Is this bug a pest or a friend?"

- The University of California at Davis has a great online IPM site, www .ipm.ucdavis.edu. Its purpose is to help people manage and identify insects, mites, diseases, nematodes, weeds, and vertebrate pests.

- The Buglady Consulting Company, at www.bugladyconsulting.com, has a great section on "Help for Homeowners on Pests" and within it a section on common pests.

- The University of Florida Pest Alerts has lots of great information on insects, diseases, and controls at entomology.ifas.ufl.edu/pestalert.

- The University of Illinois–Research Library has a great website on beneficial insects, www.library.illinois.edu/envi/beneficialinsects.html. The site is a resource guide with lots of definitions, databases, and web resources to help you understand and choose the correct beneficial insects for your yard or garden.

- The Purdue University website, http://extension.entm.purdue.edu, "Extension Entomology–Connecting You With Pest Information," has topics covering beekeeping; biological control; exotic invasive pests; fruit, landscape, and ornamental plants; and more.

- The United States Department of Agriculture website has a section on "Identification Aids & Services," which covers entomology, botany, snails, plant pathology, and nematology. You can also find links at that site to the BugGuide.Net, an online community of naturalists dedicated to learning about and sharing observations of insects, spiders, and other related creatures.

     The USDA site is www.aphis.usda.gov/plant_health/identification/ idaids.shtml.

     The USDA also provides national pest alerts at www.aphis.usda.gov/ plant_health/plant_pest_info.

LOCAL RESOURCES

Every state has local agricultural offices to help residents. Many exotic pests are first brought to the attention of officials from homeowners who have found a strange insect in their yard. Look for these offices in your local government white pages and online:

- Cooperative Extension Office
- Agricultural Extension Office
- County Department of Agriculture
- State Department of Agriculture

Master Gardener Associations are a great resource. These individuals take extensive classes to become master gardeners. In some cities, these associations take free phone calls from the public and may offer clinics with volunteers who can look at your samples of pests or affected plant material and help identify the problem. Look in your county government pages for their phone number or check to see whether the Master Gardener association in your area has a website.

Societies for specific plant categories—like the Rose Society, Native Plant Society, or Plumeria Society—have extensive knowledge of the plants they love. Many have monthly meetings and classes. These open events are usually published in the newspaper or found on their websites.

Garden clubs in your area can help with insect problems. They are familiar with gardening in your area and have probably encountered the same problems before. Look for meeting times in your local newspaper.

Your local university or community college may have an entomology or landscaping department. Consider an extension class.

Nurseries often have staffers who are well versed in the local insect population. Bring a dead sample of the insect in question to a well-established nursery. To make sure it is dead, place the insect in a plastic bag and keep it in the freezer overnight—you do not want to accidentally transport and introduce a serious pest. Some nurseries offer identification classes for their customers. Note: If the nursery staff does not know what the insect is, keep trying until you find someone who does. New exotic insects are found in the United States each year, and early detection is the key to eradication. You may save the agriculture in your area with your discovery.

SUPPLIERS OF BENEFICIAL ORGANISMS AND INSECT-MONITORING SYSTEMS

(This list comprises only a few of the companies that supply beneficial organisms or insect-monitoring systems; check your local phone book for suppliers near you.)

Before you go out and buy beneficial organisms, use the sites listed here and our Internet resources (see pages 167–68) to really get to know these insects or organisms. Use traps to see exactly what is already coming to your yard. You may have beneficial insects visiting that you are not aware of. Find out what these beneficial insects like to eat besides the pest you are trying to kill. You may find the beneficial insect you want to buy also eats something you could plant to attract it. Many beneficial insects favor composite flowers for pollen. Here are a few other things to consider before purchasing:

- Check for parasites on any pests you have. Many parasitic wasps do a great job of keeping pests in check. Look for cocoons on caterpillars, dark spots in giant whitefly egg masses, and so on. Be a good detective. If you find parasitized insect pests, leave them alone and let nature do the work.

- Have you identified the pest correctly? Double check to make sure you are purchasing the correct beneficial organism.

- Don't forget to check shipping costs. Most insects are shipped overnight, and that can add to your cost.

AlphaScents–Insect-Monitoring Systems

Two locations:
1089 Willamette Falls Drive
West Linn, OR 97068
Tel: (971) 998-8284
and
7676 Tuttle Road
Bridgeport, NY 13030
Tel: (315) 699-1991
www.alphascents.com
Supplier of quality insect-monitoring systems composed of various types of traps and lures designed to reduce toxic pesticide use.

The Beneficial Insect Company

PO Box 471143
Charlotte, North Carolina 28247
Tel: (704) 607-1631
www.thebeneficialinsectco.com
Supplier of biological insect control products in the form of beneficial insects to farmers, stables, gardeners, greenhouses, and orchards to help control pests with their natural predators.

Beneficial Insectary

Facilities in United States and Canada
9664 Tanqueray Court
Redding, CA 96003
Tel: (800) 477-3715
www.insectary.com
Suppliers of beneficial organisms.

BioLogic Company

PO Box 177
Willow Hill, PA 17271
Tel: (717) 349-2789
www.biologicco.com
Grows, formulates, and sells natural insect parasites and pathogens of pests. Also supplies natural biocontrol products for horticulture, home, lawn, garden, and greenhouse use. Online newsletter.

Gardens Alive!
 5100 Schenley Place
 Lawrenceburg, IN 47025
 Tel: (513) 354-1482
 www.gardensalive.com
 Supplier of environmentally responsible organic products for pest control, plant care, and pet care, and beneficial organisms. Free catalog, information, and online newsletter.

Grangetto's Farm & Garden Supply
 1105 W. Mission Avenue
 Escondido, CA 92025
 (three other Southern California locations)
 Tel: (800) 536-4671
 www.grangettos.com
 Full line of organic products, pest traps, and barrier products. Online newsletter and videos.

Peaceful Valley Farm Supply
 PO Box 2209
 Grass Valley, CA 95945
 Tel: (888) 784-1722
 www.groworganic.com
 Suppliers of organic products, seeds, beneficial organisms, traps, and pest control products (including gopher wire). Website has excellent informative videos.

Pest Wizard
 700 E. Redlands Boulevard, U-189
 Redlands, CA 92373
 Tel: (909) 557-4419
 www.pestwizard.com
 Suppliers of safe, nontoxic insect traps and lures. Website has great integrated pest management information.

Planet Natural

1612 Gold Avenue

Bozeman, MT 59715

Tel: (800) 289-6656

www.planetnatural.com

Supplier of natural and organic products for the home, lawn, and garden. Lots of items, including beneficial organisms, books, composting products, and pet care. Online newsletter, garden advice, and garden forum.

In Canada:

Koppert Biological Systems

50 Ironside Cres. Unit #2

Scarborough, Ontario M1X 1G4

Tel: (800) 567-4195

www.koppertonline.ca

Suppliers of beneficial insects, mites, and nematodes to control harmful insect pests in your greenhouse, solarium, garden, or lawn. Website has ID Your Pest and Ask the Expert sections.

Natural Insect Company

3737 Netherby Road

Stevensville, Ontario L0S 1S0

Tel: (905) 382-2904

www.naturalinsectcontrol.com

Environmentally friendly product supplier specializing in beneficial insects, biological pest controls, Canadian beneficial nematodes, and more. Online newsletter.

Glossary

abdomen—the posterior portion of the body.

adaptation—any genetically controlled characteristic that helps an animal to survive in its environment.

antenna—sensory appendage located on the head of an insect.

arthropods—invertebrate animals that are members of the phylum Arthropoda, including insects, arachnids, and crustaceans.

bacteria—microscopic organisms that can be parasitic or beneficial, and have round, rod, spiral, or filament-shaped cell bodies.

beak—a protruding mouth part of a sucking insect or a bird.

beneficial—a term used to describe a plant or animal that contributes to the well-being of people or nature.

biological control (biocontrol)—the use of organisms or viruses to control or reduce the numbers of parasites, weeds, or other pests.

camouflage—to act or appear like its surroundings, so it can't be seen easily.

carnivore—an organism that feeds on the flesh of other organisms.

caterpillar—the larval form of a butterfly or moth.

chemical control—method used to reduce the populations of pests with chemical solutions.

cocoon—a silken case inside which a pupa moth is formed.

cold-blooded—describes an animal whose body temperature is regulated by its surroundings rather than its body.

complete metamorphosis—a complete change in form, in the maturing process of certain insects, which involves four stages: egg to larva to pupa to adult.

crawler—the active first stage of a scale insect.

cultural control—method used to reduce the populations of pests by changing their natural surroundings.

diurnal—describes organisms that are active during the daytime.

entomologist—a person who studies insects.

entomology—the study of insects.

exoskeleton—a skeleton or supporting structure on the outside of the body.

file and scraper—a ridge and angle on the bottom surface of the front wing, near the base, used by crickets to produce sound.

food chain—sequence in which organisms feed on other organisms, including producers (plants), consumers (prey and predators), and decomposers.

frass—the debris or excrement of insects.

fumigate—to use gaseous compounds for the purpose of destroying pests.

grub—the larval form of some beetles.

habitat—the place where an organism normally lives.

hemelytron—meaning "half wing," the front wing of the order of insects called Hemiptera, or true bugs.

herbivore—an animal that eats plants.

hibernation—dormancy during the winter.

honeydew—a sweet liquid that is secreted onto the leaves of plants by aphids and other insects.

incomplete metamorphosis—a change in form during the gradual maturing process from egg to adult in insects. The egg hatches and the tiny insect that hatches looks like a miniature adult. The stages are called molts, and there is no pupal form: the insect goes from egg to nymph to adult.

instar—the stage of an insect between successive molts in incomplete metamorphosis.

integrated pest management (IPM)—a pest management strategy that examines all aspects of pest management and comes up with a comprehensive analysis of the problem, in order to produce the maximum crop yield and the minimum adverse effects to humans and the environment.

invertebrates—organisms like insects and worms that do not have a backbone.

larva—the immature stage between the egg and pupa in insects that undergo complete metamorphosis.

litter—the group of offspring born to an animal at one time.

maggot—a legless fly larva that does not have a well-developed head.

migrate—to move from one location to another for food or reproduction.

molt—a process of shedding; in insects, a process of shedding the exoskeleton.

negative reinforcement—the act of making something undesirable by associating something negative with it.

nocturnal—describing organisms that are active at night.

nymph—a stage in incomplete metamorphosis. Nymphs are immature insects that resemble tiny adults. Several molts may occur during this stage.

omnivore—an organism that feeds on both plants and flesh.

ootheca—the covering or case of an egg mass.

order—a subdivision of a class of organisms, containing a group of related families.

overwinter—to survive through the winter.

parasite—an animal that lives in or on the body of another living animal (the host) for at least part of its life. The parasite may or may not kill its host animal.

parasitoid—an organism that lives in or on a host organism and ultimately sterilizes or kills the host.

parthenogenesis—the production of offspring without fertilization.

pest—an organism (either plant or animal) that is harmful or annoying to humans.

pheromone—a substance produced by one organism that influences the behavior or physiology of another organism of the same species.

predator—an animal that attacks and feeds on other animals (prey).

proboscis—an extended mouthpart, which in insects can be beak-like or tube-like.

pupa—the stage between the larva and the adult form in insects with complete metamorphosis. This stage is nonfeeding and inactive.

quarantine—to reduce the number of pests by isolating and excluding them from certain areas.

queen—a female that is capable of reproduction in a colony of social insects.

scavenger—an animal that feeds on dead plants or animals, decaying materials, or animal wastes.

scientific name—an internationally recognized Latinized name for a species.

skeletonize—to reduce something, such as a leaf, to skeleton form.

species—a group of individual organisms that are similar in structure and physiology and are capable of reproducing fertile offspring together.

suborder—a major subdivision of an order, containing a group of related families.

thorax—the body region in insects between the head and the abdomen, which gives rise to the walking legs and wings.

torpor—a form of dormancy that is used by animals, such as hummingbirds, to conserve energy.

vector—a transmitter of disease or pathogens.

warm-blooded—describes an animal whose body temperature is regulated from within its body.

wildfly—a term to describe a fertile, nonirradiated fly.

Bibliography

Ball, Jeff, and Liz Ball. *Rodale's Landscape Problem Solver.* Emmaus, PA: Rodale Press, 1989.

Borror, Donald J., and Dwight M. DeLong. *An Introduction to the Study of Insects,* 3rd ed. New York: Holt, Rinehart and Winston, 1971.

Burt, William H., and Richard P. Grossenheider. *A Field Guide to the Mammals of America North of Mexico.* Boston: Houghton Mifflin Company, 1976.

Dadant and Sons, eds. *The Hive and the Honey Bee.* Carthage, IL: Journal Printing Company, 1975.

Debach, Paul. *Biological Control by Natural Enemies.* New York: Cambridge University Press, 1979.

Ellis, Barbara W., and Fern Marshall Bradley. *The Organic Gardener's Handbook of Natural Insect and Disease Control.* Emmaus, PA: Rodale Press, 1996.

Fichter, George S. *Insect Pests.* New York: Golden Press, 1966.

Flint, Mary Louise. *Pests of the Garden and Small Farm.* Oakland, CA: Division of Agriculture and Natural Resources, University of California, 1990.

Garden Pests & Diseases. Menlo Park, CA: Sunset Publishing Co., 1993.

Gay, Kathlyn. *Cleaning Nature Naturally.* New York: Walker and Company, 1991.

Grainger, Janette, and Connie Moore. *Natural Insect Repellents.* Austin, TX: The Herb Bar, 1991.

Kerr Kitchen. *Pantry.* Los Angeles: Consumer Products Division of Kerr Group, Inc., 1995.

Kilgore, Wendell W., and Richard L. Doutt. *Pest Control: Biological, Physical, and Selected Chemical Methods.* New York: Academic Press, 1967.

Marer, Patrick J. *The Safe and Effective Use of Pesticides.* Oakland, CA: Division of Agriculture and Natural Resources, University of California, 1988.

Metcalf, C. L., and W. P. Flint. *Destructive and Useful Insects.* New York: McGraw-Hill Book Company, 1962.

Nancarrow, Loren, and Janet Hogan Taylor. *Dead Daisies Make Me Crazy.* Berkeley, CA: Ten Speed Press, 2000.

Orr, Robert T. *Vertebrate Biology.* Philadelphia: W. B. Saunders Company, 1971.

Pleasant, Barbara. *The Gardener's Bug Book.* Pownal, VT: Storey Publishing, 1994.

Pringle, Laurence. *Pests and People.* New York: Macmillan Publishing Co., 1972.

Routhier, William. *Africanized Honey Bee Reference Manual.* San Diego, CA: California Department of Food and Agriculture, 1994.

Tyrrell, Ester Quesada. *Hummingbirds: Their Life and Behavior.* New York: Crown Publishers, 1985.

Unitt, Philip. *The Birds of San Diego County.* San Diego, CA: San Diego Society of Natural History, 1984.

Western Garden Problem Solver. Menlo Park, CA: Sunset Publishing Corporation, 1998.

INTERNET RESOURCES

California Department of Food and Agriculture
www.cdfa.ca.gov

Iowa State Entomology Department
www.ent.iastate.edu

National Pesticide Information Center

www.npic.orst.edu

Organic Gardens@Suite 101

www.suite101.com/jamie-mcintosh

Pest Wizard

www.pestwizard.com

Purdue University, "Extension Entomology—Connecting You With Pest Information"

www.extension.entm.purdue.edu

The BugGuide.Net

www.bugguide.net

The Buglady Consulting Company

www.bugladyconsulting.com

University of California at Davis, IPM (Integrated Pest Management)

www.ipm.ucdavis.edu

University of Florida Pest Alerts

www.entomology.ifas.ufl.edu/pestalert

University of Illinois—Research Library, on beneficial insects

www.library.illinois.edu/envi/beneficialinsects.html

United States Department of Agriculture, "Identification Aids & Services"

www.aphis.usda.gov/plant_health/identification/idaids.shtml

United State Department of Agriculture Pest Alerts

www.aphis.usda.gov/plant_health/plant_pest_info

US Environmental Protection Agency

www.epa.gov

Weekend Gardener

www.weekendgardener.net

What's That Bug?

www.whatsthatbug.com

About the Authors

As one of the country's first environmental TV reporters, Loren Nancarrow has seen interest and knowledge in humans' role in the natural environment grow significantly in the past three decades, and he's been awarded some of broadcast journalism's highest honors for reporting on environmental science and nature around the planet. When not covering the news, Loren has worked at improving the environment as a founding trustee of the EcoLife Foundation. The EcoLife Foundation has projects in the United States, Mexico, and Africa aimed at reducing carbon output, reforesting important habitat, and saving vulnerable species, like monarch butterflies in Mexico and mountain gorillas in Uganda. Loren makes his home in coastal Southern California. He and his wife, Susie, have three grown children. He is a passionate organic vegetable gardener.

A native Californian, Janet Hogan Taylor graduated from San Jose State University with a bachelor's degree in biology with emphasis in entomology. Janet took a job with the San Diego Zoo, where she became a senior keeper in the bird department. Never forgetting her roots in entomology, Janet helped develop several natural pest control techniques at the zoo to keep the birds and animals pest free. Currently, Janet works as an environmental scientist and resides in Southern California with her husband, a black lab named Drake, and hundreds of backyard birds, reptiles, and assorted varmints. She and her husband Brian, also an entomologist, have two grown children.

Loren and Janet have written three books together: *Dead Snails Leave No Trails*, *Dead Daisies Make Me Crazy*, and *The Worm Book*.

Index